Publishing Imprint: Women Alive Ministries
All rights reserved.

This book is intended for both small group and individual reading.

To order this book go to www.cometothefire.org

Library of Congress Cataloging in Publication Data:
ISBN 978-0-9800033-0-7
Printed in the United States of America

10 9 8 7 6 5 4 3 2 1

~ Obstacle Five: My Faith Seems Too Small.

~ Obstacle Six: I've Never Received Evangelism Training.

~ Obstacle Seven: I'm Fearful of Getting Rejected.

~

Obstacle One: I'm Not an Evangelist.

"Christ's love compels us, because
we are convinced that one died for all."

2 Corinthians 5:14

*Evangelism is not a professional job for a few trained
men, but is the unrelenting responsibility of every
person who belongs to the company of Jesus.*
—Elton Trueblood

A Divine Appointment

Pamela Enderby

*"And he died for all, that those who live should no
longer live for themselves" (2 Corinthians 5:15).*

"I can't begin to evangelize my neighbors. I don't have
enough time to save my own kids." When this spiritually
respected mom voiced her honest concerns during an outreach planning meeting, my heart applauded her. I didn't
agree out loud, though, because I was the pastor's wife—
someone expected to help support and cultivate evangelism.

For years I kept secret my string of "legitimate excuses" for ignoring the Great Commission. Sure, hearing
Jesus' words made me occasionally twinge, "Go and make
disciples of all nations, baptizing them in the name of the
Father and of the Son and of the Holy Spirit, and teaching
them to obey everything I have commanded you" (Matthew
28:19-20). Nevertheless, I could justify my excuses.

Excuse # 1 Only ministers and designated missionaries assigned to foreign countries evangelize. I had dismissed the caring insurance salesman in a small Wisconsin farming community who shared the gospel with my husband and me.

Excuse # 2 How could God use my shy nature to bring anyone to repentance?

Excuse # 3 I thought to do the work of an evangelist, I needed to have the "gift of evangelism."

Excuse # 4 Living a consistent lifestyle of kindness and unconditional love toward unbelievers (known as lifestyle evangelism) sounded exhausting. Caring for my five children and my husband already kept my plate full.

Then unexpectedly, God's grace and mercy for the lost stepped in to change my mind and my heart. My excuses unraveled when my friend asked me to pray for Jami, her pregnant future daughter-in-law, a high school senior. Little did I know that committing to pray for Jami would crack the door open to my first outreach journey.

I asked God to steer Jami away from abortion and toward adoption. The more I prayed, the more compassion grew in my heart for her.

When I finally met Jami at a picnic, six months later, she felt more like a sister than a stranger. Prayer had bridged our age gap and paved a path for building our friendship.

A few nights later, God's familiar nudge awakened me from a deep sleep. I had grown familiar with His wake-up calls. Settling into my favorite living room recliner, I mumbled my usual complaint. "I'm so tired. Did I have to get up?" Of course, I didn't have to, but I have learned over the years that when I obey God's early morning invitations, we enjoy sweet intimacy.

As I closed my eyes, Jami's face clearly came to mind. "God, please bring her to salvation."

Then with my eyes still closed something unusual happened. I pictured Jami and me sitting in a booth at my favorite Italian restaurant talking about God.

Just as quickly, Jami's face disappeared. I opened my eyes and pondered the vision. Hmm ... could God possibly want me to share my faith with her? Immediately, fear gripped me. I hardly knew her! I didn't want to turn her off!

"You're just imagining this," a silent voice mocked. "You'll make a fool of yourself. You don't know how to evangelize." For the next half hour, I seriously entertained the adversary's lies.

"O.K. I'll forget it," I moaned. But, as I remained curled up on the couch, thoughts of meeting with Jami kept returning.

Finally, I called out to God for help. "God, I believe You want me to witness to Jami because You love her and want her saved. I'll do it, but I need Your help. I'm afraid. Please help me!"

Once I relinquished my will, His presence welled up within me, exchanging my misery with His strength.

My enemy quietly bowed out, carrying his lies with him, and the battle ended. I crawled back into bed at peace, yet full of anticipation.

The following morning I phoned Jami. After warming up to her with small talk, I threw out a fleece. "Hey, Jami, do you like Italian food?"

"It's my favorite. My mother is Italian." My confidence soared. Wow! God really is in this, I thought.

Within a few days I met Jami at The Olive Garden and to my amazement the waiter seated us at the same table I pictured during my prayer time. This is like playing follow the leader. God leads; I follow. I began to relax and even enjoy this adventure.

When we finished our meal, I knew the time had come to share my spiritual journey with Jami. I didn't have Scriptures memorized to share, nor did I have the plan of salvation down pat. I simply shared from my heart my life experiences.

When I reached the point of explaining my hunger for God as a teenager, sadness filled Jami's deep brown eyes.

"God knows you, too, and cares for you, Jami," I said, tenderly.

A tear trickled down her cheek. "I've recently been thinking a lot about God. I want to know Him better. I think this is what I need." Jami's receptivity stimulated our conversation. Perhaps at that point I could have invited her to ask Jesus into her heart, but she caught me off guard, so quickly admitting her need for Christ. *Getting Jami saved can't possibly be this easy,* I thought. *Especially not in a restaurant!*

After I paid the bill we stepped outside and lingered in the parking lot. I made awkward small talk, sensing we had unfinished business, but I didn't know the next step. I wished I had known salvation Scriptures to share, but to be honest, the thrill of meeting with Jami and seeing her hunger for God so overwhelmed me I probably would have forgotten them!

Just then the tract I had tucked in my purse came to mind. "Here, Jami, if you read this, I think it will help you find God." She smiled, and politely accepted it.

The next day Jami called to tell me she had read the tract and prayed the "sinner's prayer" printed on the back. "Is there anything else I need to do?" Her voice sounded light and alive.

Jami's decision to receive Christ as Savior sent my spirit soaring. Regaining my composure, I calmly replied, "You need to nurture your new relationship with Christ by reading the Bible. Begin reading the gospel of John, the fourth book of the New Testament." Before hanging up the phone, we set a date to meet again. I wanted to be sure Jami got started on the right foot and followed through.

For days I rejoiced over Jami's salvation, and I marveled at how simple and how much fun it was to share my faith. With my evangelistic appetite soaring, I intentionally built more relationships. If I sensed someone needed Jesus, I prayerfully reached out to that person.

My first opportunity happened at the grocery store. By initiating friendly conversations with the same cashier, I grew to know her needs and interests. Over the course of a year we enjoyed bike rides together, attended baseball games together, and invited our kids to one another's birthday parties. Eventually, I had opportunities to pray with her and share the Gospel. One day, after she and her family had moved to Canada, she called to tell me she had received Christ as her Savior.

I aimed at getting to know my elderly neighbor, a widower. I cooked him an occasional dinner, invited him to our house for special occasions, and eventually shared the gospel with him. Three days before he died, he prayed to receive Christ.

Giving small gifts or cards to my kids' teachers also planted outreach seeds. By just being myself and touching the lost in simple ways, I watched God transform hearts.

Meanwhile, the demands of motherhood continued to scream for my attention. Making meals, doing laundry, cleaning house, and keeping appointments threatened to damper evangelism. Trying to embrace the lost amidst caring for daily needs and concerns brought me to my knees. I began to pray about everything. "Lord, I give my time, talents, and resources to you. Order my steps. Help me to do nothing more and nothing less than what you call me to do." By daily submitting my agenda to God, I found myself reordering my priorities. I let go of some tasks and postponed others in order to invest time in loving others to Jesus.

Prayer plays the key part in keeping my heart tender and teachable. When I detect I'm growing indifferent toward unbelievers, I cry out to God, asking Him to enlarge and soften my heart again. By giving Him access, He creates a channel for His unyielding love to flow in me and through me. I also ask God to help me see evangelism as a privilege, not another thing I have to do. When I see the lost through His eyes, reaching out happens more naturally.

Jesus said, "Go and make disciples of all nations." Now I'm convinced it's possible for busy moms like me to evangelize. I simply must be myself and use simple, consistent outreach efforts, done in God's way and in His time and in His strength. It's turning out to be a lot of fun!

Discussion Questions

1. It is true that God has given certain people the "gift of evangelism," those who motivate, train, and equip others to do the work of an evangelist. All Christians, though, are called to evangelize. Compare Ephesians 4:11 which speaks of the gift of evangelism with Matthew 10:32 which speaks of those called to evangelize.

2. Accepting our God-given responsibilities without concern about our limitations teaches us to depend totally upon Him. What well-meaning, logical excuses have kept you from evangelizing?

3. Read Ephesians 3:15-21. How can you be empowered to do what appears impossible? What resources are you available to you? What evangelistic results can you expect?

4. Also, consider Philippians 4:13 and 2 Corinthians 12:9. How will embracing these truths help you defeat your outreach excuses?

5. "Outreach apathy" can easily sneak into our hearts. How will you guard yourself from it?"

Evangelism is one beggar telling another beggar
where to get bread. —C. H. Spurgeon

My Profession Is My Fishing Net

Raymond "Doc" Fletcher as told to Pamela Enderby

"A friend loves at all times" (Proverbs 17:17).

I'm an area manager for a large foods manufacturer that sells and distributes beverages and snacks to convenience stores. I first met Butch, my coworker, when I was transferred from Texas to Kansas City in 1995. Butch and I had nothing in common. We worked for different divisions of the company that were highly competitive; he was rearing a young family; my kids were grown and living out of state. Our biggest difference was that Butch partied hard and played hard. I had left that scene several years earlier.

One day I mentioned to my wife Nancy my desire to get acquainted with him. "It's ridiculous that we work for the same company, live in the same town, and talk only every five or six months or see each other only once a year at a company football game." I seriously heeded Ecclesiastes 11:4. "Whoever watches the wind will not plant; whoever looks at the clouds will not reap." Waiting for all conditions to be favorable to bridge a friendship with him seemed foolish. I didn't have any intention to lead Butch to salvation because I didn't consider myself an evangelist. However, I had hoped God could use me to help prepare the path.

"Sure, that will be great," Butch responded to my lunch invitation. We had lunch together twice that year and talked about nothing but business.

During the following two years I watched from a distance as Butch's life spiraled downward. His hard-partying, hard-playing lifestyle reminded me of my ugly past, although I had done a lot worse and played a lot harder. I could see Butch masking his pain and I hoped nothing really bad would happen to him. I figured preaching to him would only make him run faster from the truth like I did during my drinking days.

In 1997, I had a tremendous sales year. My wife prayed I'd find favor with God and man, and I did. I'd wake up with fresh business ideas every morning, which led to winning regional and national sales contests. It felt like winning the Triple Crown and never breaking sweat. Because of my success, I gained Butch's respect.

Finally, a crisis came that opened a door for my wife and me to touch Butch with Jesus' love. Vickki, Butch's wife, had just given birth to triplets, and she needed surgery because her hipbone was partially dead. Butch feared for her life.

One evening I phoned Butch. "Nancy and I bought a sack of new clothes for your babies, and I want to deliver them. Will you meet me half way from your house to my house?

In the parking lot of a strip mall, Butch and I exchanged a firm handshake. Deep lines were etched across his forehead. "How is Vickki?" I asked.

While Butch explained his wife's debilitating disease, he fought back tears. For the first time, I could see Butch helpless and vulnerable.

"How can we help you?" I offered. "Some ladies from our church would be happy to pitch in by helping with housecleaning and making some meals." The hard lines on Butch's forehead softened.

"May I pray for you?" I asked.

"Yes, you may pray," he replied.

"If it's all right, I'll just pray for you right now," I said.

Standing beside the car, we bowed our heads. Butch's body shook with grief as I began to pray for his wife's health. I held him in my arms as we cried together.

I left with a strong desire to contact Butch more frequently. About every two weeks, I'd call to check on Vickki's condition and assure him of our prayers. After a year of phone contacts, we met for lunch a second time.

Sauntering into the Chinese restaurant I didn't expect our conversation to go much beyond the usual kids, family, and business. But Butch didn't stop there. Halfway into lunch he leaned over the table and peered into my eyes. "I think I can trust you. I think you'll tell me the truth." Like a hurting child searching for comfort, he paused and quietly added, "I have what feels like a hole in my heart, and I don't know what to do about it."

I was totally blown away. Butch's macho image had finally melted and he let down his guard. After I had prayed for three years for this man and his wife, he expressed his need for Jesus.

"Absolutely," I responded and carefully gathered my thoughts. "All of us need a Savior. We need to recognize that we are sinners. Jesus can save you and mend your heart."

"That's exactly what I need," he confessed. "What do I do now?"

"Think about this and if you believe it, ask Jesus to be your Savior." I added. "Go to the Christian bookstore and ask for a study Bible. Start with the book of John and read the notes. They'll give historical background."

Within a few weeks, Butch and I met again. "The most amazing thing happened," he said. "When I was in my hotel room in Oklahoma City, I woke up early one morning, crying. They were tears of pure sadness over how I had offended God. So I began repenting for my sins," he explained. Then he added, "After repenting, I started crying again. But this time, they were tears of absolute joy. I never had so much fun crying in all my life."

Since Butch's conversion, his family relationships are radically changed. "I used to feel I had to spend time with Brooke, my 8-year-old daughter, but now I want to. I enjoy strolling through the park with her, counting the flowers together, and admiring the birds and trees. We have a whole new relationship," he laughed, jubilantly.

Butch also devours God's Word. Within a few months he read all the Gospels, Acts, Romans, and Ephesians twice. One day while reading his Bible, Vickki wrapped her arms around him and praised him, "I'm so proud of what you're doing." Although she still views Christianity as nothing more than church going, she's discovering that Butch's positive changes are linked to God.

Today, with God at the center of our relationship, Butch has become one of my closest friends. When we meet for our three-hour lunches, we encourage one another with spiritual truths and cry tears of joy over God's goodness.

I've never been the hard-selling type of businessman and I don't use that approach with my coworkers to present the Gospel. But when opportunity knocks, soft selling the Truth is by far the most exciting and rewarding part of my job. I simply wait for God to lead me to my coworkers' islands of concerns and needs and then share Christ as Lord in that context.

Even if my coworkers seem like the most unlikely people to get saved, I'm now convinced that God's love has the power to bridge our widest differences.

Discussion Questions

1. Although, like many of us, Raymond didn't regard himself an "evangelist," do you think his approach with Butch was any less effective?

2. Do you face relationship differences with your co-workers? Explain.

3. "Always be prepared to give an answer to everyone who asks you to give the reason for the hope that you have" (1 Peter 3:15). What would you say to a coworker who has questions about your faith?

4. Ask the Lord to help you overlook personal differences with your coworkers and fill you with His love so that you might begin to build bridges.

Cultivate a buoyant sense of the crowded kindnesses of God in your daily life. —Alexander MacLaren

Road Tested Witnessing

Stephanie Fridley as told to Pamela Enderby

"Rejoice in the Lord you who are righteous and praise his holy name" (Psalm 97:12).

An early morning rainfall in Westchester, California, spiked the air with the scent of orange blossoms. I closed my eyes and inhaled deeply. The sweet aroma seemed to quench my thirsty soul and awaken my spirit with thanksgiving.

I poured out a steady stream of praises for my family, friends, and, most of all, my salvation while driving to work. That left no room for entertaining my usual cares and concerns.

By late afternoon, even after putting in a full day's work, joy still had its grip on me and I longed to share it. If the usual vendor with long brown hair and baggy jeans was selling roses at the island intersection on Pacific Coast Highway, I planned to splurge and buy a bunch. *This hippy-*

looking guy surely needs a touch of kindness today, too, I thought. *Perhaps I can say something that will make him aware of God's sweet grace.* In the past, we exchanged only small talk while I waited for the signal light to turn.

Now, approaching the red light, I rolled down my window and cleared my throat, exercising a new confidence in Jesus' promise: I will give you what to say (Matthew 10:19-20).

To my surprise, the red light turned green and the traffic flow speeded up. Hadn't God prepared me for this moment? I questioned. I really want to show him that God cares for him, too! Slightly bewildered and disappointed, I made an alternative, snap decision. I'll just throw him a friendly wave and talk with him tomorrow. Yet, that strong inner desire to say something meaningful, something significant, remained.

Instead of speeding up with the traffic, I slowed down. Easing forward at a snail's pace, I quickly turned my thoughts upward and inquired of the One who knows exactly what to say. "Now what?"

Without hearing an audible voice, I acted upon impulse and took a sharp left turn. Poking my smiling face out the window, I shouted. "God loves you!" I could feel the power of this simple, age-old message.

Glancing in my rearview mirror, the vendor was flashing me a bright smile. Evidently, he heard me and received the blessing! Maybe that's the first time he had heard someone tell him, "God loves you!" I thought. My joy increased.

Now, in the midst of busy, bumper-to-bumper rush hour traffic, God's plan continued to unfold with another surprise. He gently whispered, "I love you, Stephanie. You are precious to me." God's tender words arrested my attention. Over the years, I had learned to recognize His voice, and now, once again, I felt His love. Tears trickled down my cheeks. I'm learning that opening my heart's door wide to do small kind deeds ignites inner joy. If I let someone go ahead of me in line at the grocery store, tell my mailman, "Thanks for doing a good job," or bake cookies for my elderly neighbor, God's love shines. With each opportunity to spread a little sunshine in someone's heart, I experience the truth of Jesus' words, "It is more blessed to give than to receive" (Acts 20:35).

Discussion Questions

1. Joy compelled Stephanie's witness. Where does joy come from?

2. Oftentimes, we lose the joy of our salvation because we forget what we've been saved from! Pause for a moment and think about what your life might be like if you had not come to Christ. What did Jesus save you from?

3. Explain a time when the joy of Christ was so full in your life that it led into an evangelistic opportunity.

4. Proverbs 11: 24 states, "One man gives freely but gains even more." What did Stephanie unexpectedly gain as a result of freely sharing her joy?

5. "We are the first account of the gospel most people will ever read," states Jim Petersen. God's love and joy expressed through Stephanie made her stand out. What makes you stand out?

Ninety-percent of evangelism is love.
—Dr. Bob Smith

From Ditch Digging to Wiggly Pre-Schoolers

Richard Harris as told to Pamela Enderby

"Let each generation tell its children of your mighty acts" (Psalm 145:4 NLT).

On Sunday morning, at the crack of dawn, I awaken, anticipating the fun and challenges of teaching a bunch of bright-eyed pre-schoolers. Their warm hugs and cheery smiles always revitalize me after working an arduous week of heavy construction and landscaping.

One Sunday School class shines in my mind. Five-year-old Zachary greeted me in his usual manner, smiling as he rushed into my open arms. Then instead of darting off to play, as usual, he stood before me, at attention, still like a soldier.

Observing his white shirt and bow tie, I proclaimed, "Zachary, you look just like a preacher today!" He smiled proudly. "I think you are going to be a preacher," I added with more gusto. "You know the Good News, don't you,

Zachary?" His sparkling eyes stayed glued to mine, while he twirled his curly red hair. "The Good News is that Jesus loves you and He loves me, too."

After seating the children at their tables, I quieted them by holding my finger close to my lips. When silence fell, I shouted, "Zachary's got some Good News! Tell them, Zachary."

He bolted from his seat to a standing position.

"God loves me and He loves you, too!" he exclaimed.

"That's right, Zachary," I said, patting his shoulder.

Zachary's announcement set the stage for more "Good News." Each Sunday I allow the children a special time to share what's happening in their lives. Their heartfelt stories offer me glimpses of how God is working in their hearts. Hearing bad news, such as their pets dying or a grandma's illness, gives me opportunity to acknowledge their feelings, reinforce God's love for each one, and pray for them.

Kneeling, with our hands folded, we talk to God as our friend. Some kids pray out loud; others don't, but when we finish praying, the whole class chimes in, "Amen!" The children learn about God's love and faithfulness as they watch Him answer prayer.

Every week I set aside time to prayerfully prepare my Sunday school lesson. In addition to using standard Sunday school curriculum, I ask the Lord to give simple, creative ideas to help make our Bible story come alive.

One morning, I plopped a towel on my head and secured it with a headband. With my fake white beard and flashlight in hand, I instructed the children to trail behind me in the dark classroom. I feigned Moses leading the wandering Israelites; my flashlight symbolized the pillar of fire. Role-playing stimulates children's interest and helps them remember their Bible lesson.

Teaching my wiggly pre-schoolers is an easy and comfortable way for me to evangelize, and I wouldn't trade it for anything else. In my eyes, pre-schoolers resemble tender shoots of flowers, reaching for light—God's light. Encouragement, smiles, focused attention, and Bible stories cause blossoms of kindness and love to grow in their lives. In time, I think they will look more beautiful than any flower garden I've ever planted.

Watching godliness grow in my students' lives thrills me, but I have to admit, I'm just as delighted when my former students return and whisper in my ear, "I wish you could still be my Sunday School teacher."

Discussion Questions

1. What grownups made a positive, spiritual influence because they shared "Good News" with you when you were a child? Explain.

2. Refer to Psalm 145:4. What "mighty acts" of God have you recently shared with your children?

3. The Greek word for evangelism means "Good News." Sunday school teachers have multiple opportunities to share "Good News" with unsaved children; however, communicating on their level is key. In order to speak in a language they can understand, avoid using religious words like, "saved," "grace," "sin," "faith," "justified," "born again" or "redeemed." Write a definition for these words in terms an unbelieving child can understand.

4. Role-play leading a child to Christ. One person plays the Christian and another the child.

Running Ahead of the Spirit

Pamela Enderby

*"If we live by the Spirit, let us also walk by the
spirit" (Galatians 5:25 NASB).*

It seemed like the perfect summer day. Anna and I ped-
dled our bikes through Shawnee Mission Park. I purposely
planned this special "mother-daughter" outing to chat with
Anna about some unique challenges she might face entering third grade.

Heading toward a fork on the bike trail, I called, "Turn
to the left. I see a pretty resting spot." Anna steered her bike
around a sharp curve and raced out of sight.

From a distance, I spotted Anna leaning against a
bench, talking with a 50ish year-old woman. "Oh no," I
groaned, and slowed my pace. Anna's talkative, out-going
personality easily lends itself to friendly conversations with
strangers. She has the gift of gab, just like her dad! It appeared our precious "alone time" had come to a halt.

Peddling on, my thoughts shifted to my morning prayer. Under the sweet conviction of the Holy Spirit, I had asked God to open my eyes again to recognize outreach opportunities and restore my love for the lost. When I received Christ almost 15 years earlier, I possessed a hunger to share my faith; however, over the years, while trying to fulfill the responsibilities of rearing five children, it gradually dwindled. Now, remembering my prayer, I thought, *Perhaps God is using this outing as an outreach opportunity.*

The longer I entertained this notion, the more I convinced myself that God had planted this woman on my path to hear the Good News. Anticipation replaced my frustration. Viewing this woman as my witnessing target, I charged ahead and silently rehearsed salvation Scriptures. My palms began to turn sweaty.

The neatly dressed, well-groomed woman greeted me with a warm, bright smile as I parked my bike. Although her friendliness calmed my outreach jitters, it caused me to question my intention because I anticipated witnessing to someone with an obvious look of need for Jesus. Instead, this woman appeared calm, wearing one of those friendly grins that makes everyone feel at ease.

I resolved to push ahead with small talk. *Eventually it will lead to a spiritual conversation,* I thought. But before I could say a word, she began chatting about her favorite hiking places, her beloved golden lab, and the neighborhood children whom she loves. I simply smiled and nodded. When she finished talking, she rose from the bench, cheerfully said "good-bye," and strolled down the path. I stood motionless. The opportunity to witness never happened. My plan had failed. My idea collapsed. I didn't have the chance to speak even one kind word!

What was that all about? For a moment, I resolved to put witnessing on the shelf ... forever! I had prayed for an outreach opportunity and figured this was it. Obviously, I'm not an evangelist, I grumbled. Then I scolded myself. You should have been more assertive!

Again, ignoring the Lord of the Harvest and my disappointment, I devised another plan. When I catch up with her, I'll say something like, "Have a great day. God loves you!" Then my imagination ran wild with an interchange of leading her to Christ.

"Let's go!" I ordered Anna, pointing toward my target. Peddling slowly, I practiced my introductory lines.

Fortunately, before reaching her and embarrassing myself, God redirected me. I "heard" His inaudible command, "Pray for her salvation."

Didn't I ask for an opportunity to share my faith? I questioned.

God's command came not only as a surprise but also as a disappointment. For a moment, I considered His words, but I didn't want to admit the truth that only He knew what this woman needed because only He could really see what was going on in her heart.

I tossed out my well-meaning outreach plan and yielded to God. I asked Him to draw this woman to the Holy Spirit, convict her of sin and speak to her through other believers. When I relinquished my soul-winning intentions, my disappointment turned to peace.

Henry Blackaby says, "As instruments, we should always be in tune to God's leading. The act of evangelism is a process, and the One who initiates that process knows exactly what instrument should be played at which time. As Christians, our job is to be ready to be utilized in the symphony of evangelism."

On reflection, it's obvious I ignored the Master conductor's initial instructions. Human wisdom overruled His divine plans. But I learned an important lesson. The next time I'm inclined to run ahead of the Holy Spirit and jump to my own conclusions, I'll slow down first and consider how vitally involved He is in my evangelistic efforts. God will never execute a plan that hinders the Great Commission to seek and save the lost.

God brings everyone to Himself in accordance with His will, in His time. My job is to cooperate in the work He is already doing in their lives. I am to simply listen, obey, and trust. For now, I'm heeding His voice and playing the instrument of prayer.

Discussion Questions

1. As someone once said, "Not all the fruit on the tree is ripe for picking." How can we know if we are running ahead of God's harvest schedule?

2. Have you ever felt compelled to say "something spiritual" but instead of exposing the Gospel, you imposed it upon someone? What were the consequences?

3. Henry Blackaby refers to Christians as God's "instruments." If He initiates when, where, and how He will use us for outreach, what is our responsibility?

4. What presumptions do we sometimes make that cause misguided outreach action?

5. Why should we never consider results or possible effects to determine if we are or are not an evangelist?

*Anyone can be a soul-winner who is willing to pay
the price. —Robert Sumner*

Around the World and Back,
Again and Again

Sherry Fowler

*"The righteous is a guide to his neighbor" (Proverbs 12:26
NASB).*

After seven rewarding years of missionary adventures,
God pointed me back home. The unknown taunted me,
"Everyone in America has heard the Gospel. You're taking
steps backward if you return. What can you do there?" I
fought God's nudging for six months before surrendering. I
thought that if I didn't share my faith on foreign soil, I
wasn't doing the work of a real evangelist. Simultaneously,
I feared that if I disobeyed and remained as a missionary,
God would withhold His blessings.

Now in America, and two temporary jobs later, I was
offered a position as a "finance girl" for a car dealership. I
accepted the job, hoping it would get my foot in the door
for future employment elsewhere.

The first day of work, Suci introduced herself wearing a bright smile. Her welcoming spirit started our friendship off on the right foot, and she eventually became my mentor.

One day I asked, "Suci, where does your name come from?"

"Indonesia. I grew up there." During our lunch breaks, Indonesia became a common topic of interest since I had lived in the Netherlands and learned of its Dutch influence on Indonesia. I began to see glimpses of why God had brought me back to America and placed me at this particular job.

One day Suci explained that when she turned twenty-four she married and gave birth to Liana. She then accounted for her husband's absence. "We separated. He cannot conquer his drug addiction. I won't have that influence around Liana."

As Suci grew to trust me, she shared more intimate information about her husband. "He found 'solace' in the arms of my former coworker." Suci detailed how this scheming woman abandoned the finance team after the affair developed and then used her influence to smear Suci's good name.

Eventually I heard coworkers gossiping about Suci. She tried combating the buzzing rumors, but they still stung her to the core. God opened my eyes to Suci's pain, and He led me to see my new "mission field" in America while filling my heart with compassion for Suci.

"How can I hold back what I know to be Suci's freedom, refuge, and helping hand? How can I choose job security over someone's soul?" Day after day, I drove to work praying, "God show me how to witness to Suci. Let Your truth speak louder than her problems and her ambition. Please set Suci free."

The appropriate time came. Business had slowed, which meant Suci and I could share an office to use our multi-task skills of talking and filing.

"I was reared Catholic … with some cultural add-ons," Suci shared one day. "Once in the U.S., I chose to remember only enough to speak the same religious language as my family and teach Liana good morals. I know God is good, but I've made too many mistakes to get His help."

Suci added, "Right before my mother arrived to help with Liana, a pastor's wife invited me to church. For mom's sake, we visit. I enjoy the positive message." Her head nodded as if to agree there was something special there.

She then asked, "What do you believe? You call yourself a 'Believer in Christ'?"

I was ready to share my faith while Suci sat ready to listen. "I believe that once you choose to believe with your heart that God raised Jesus from the dead and confess with your mouth that Jesus Christ is your Lord, you become His." I stressed, "Suci, Christ's sacrifice was not only payment for our sins, but also a gift of healing. God loves you. He wants to set you free."

Suci's smile replaced itself with a gaze of wonder. She digested her thoughts out loud. "I know humor is my shield, but you seem to have peace protecting you. Customers never make you bitter … You always find the best in situations … And this, you are saying, is because God leads you?"

"That's what the cross is about, Suci. Setting your sights on what really matters. All you have to do is ask Jesus into your heart."

The next day, Suci opened the office door with a glimpse of hope. "I prayed to Jesus last night. It felt good," she said calmly. I nodded with delight.

Suci used our down time at work to ask questions about a believer's lifestyle, baptism, and the Bible's view on marriage. I pulled the Bible from my purse, showing her exactly what Scripture said. I dared to ask, "Do you want to pray together? We can ask for God's hand to correct your problems."

Suci's eyes glanced over the car lot. "Yes. I want Liana to have a father. Somehow I still love him. Is God powerful enough to get through to my husband?"

I quoted, "With God, all things are possible."

As days passed, Suci's dark eyes filled with light, bringing new life to her smiles. After lengthy consideration, she even decided to be baptized. I jumped with praise for my maturing sister in Christ. At the ceremony I gave her a Bible and invited her to my weekly Bible study. For two months we interceded for Suci's husband and marriage before he moved back in.

Suci's miraculous reports strengthened our faith. "My husband returned sober and humbled. God is teaching me to forgive him and the other woman. We are regaining each other's trust … I feel stretched, but healed. I know God is bringing my family back together." In gratitude she turned to me, "Thank you for letting God bring you into the dealership so He could show me the light I've been waiting for."

A year has passed since Suci and I left the dealership, but we still remain friends. I'm enjoying a new job at a credit union while Suci is a full-time student and mother. Her husband is trying to land a career.

Suci called the other day. "My husband and I still attend marriage counseling. He is finding victory from his own chains in a specialized support group, and I joined a woman's Bible study. Liana even bears witness to God's healing our family. Remember how she was uncomfortable around her father? Well now she holds both our hands as we pray, and with joy announces 'Amen.' She brings us thankful smiles each time."

Discussion Questions

1. We sometimes think the only "significant" work for God is behind the pulpit or on foreign soil. Why is it

difficult to accept our role as "missionaries" when we haven't left the country?

2. Identify your "mission field." Where is it and who are you evangelizing?

3. Although the car dealership kept a tight reign on its employees, Sherry remained a light in that dark place. How did she accomplish that without losing her job?

4. Discuss other ways believers can "walk as children of light" (Ephesians 5:8), even if they're not allowed to talk about Christianity while at their workplaces?

5. Author Richard Foster believes "we are responsible before God to pray for those that He brings into our circle of nearness." Who in your circle of nearness needs your prayers today?

~

Obstacle Two: I'm Too Busy; I'm Too Tired!

"May our Lord Jesus Christ Himself and God our Father, who loved us and by His grace gave us eternal encouragement and good hope, encourage your hearts and strengthen you in every good deed and word."

(2 Thessalonians 2:16-17)

*If you give of yourself physically you become
exhausted, but if you give of yourself spiritually, you
get more strength. —Oswald Chambers*

Running Ragged
At Wal-Mart

Greg Hughes as told to Pamela Enderby

*"But we have this treasure in jars of clay to show that this
all-surpassing power is from God" (2 Corinthians 4:7).*

I got stuck in a mile long checkout line at Wal-Mart. To
make matters worse, a tall macho guy planted himself behind me and was breathing down my neck, cussing like
crazy at the cashier. "Man, they're making so much #*!^%
money off us. Why don't they open more registers?"

The last thing I wanted to hear was more griping. I had
just finished a long weekend of drama training with 20
teenagers, preparing them for a mission's trip. Their com-
plaints dragged me down. "Do I have to wear my cos-
tume?" "When do we eat lunch?" "My make-up looks
weird." "I miss my boyfriend." "I'm hungry."

Standing in line, I juggled an armful of baby-wipes,
batteries, electrical tape, Imodium, Ex-Lax, and a first-aid

kit. My balancing act aroused the impatient customer's interest. "What are you doing?" he boomed. If there had been an escape route, I would have run.

If I ignore this dude, he might get hot headed and spout off at me, I thought. So I replied, "I'm taking a bunch of students to Lima, Peru. They'll present a drama there that tells a story about Jesus." I enunciated the name of Jesus, loud and clear, hoping that using the "J word" would turn him off. Instead, he shifted his weight, and blurted out, "Why are you doing that?"

I replied simply, "Well, the Bible tells us to go into the entire world to tell people about Jesus. So we're going!"

"So, what's your drama about?" he persisted.

Since the line continued moving slowly I accepted the fact this guy wasn't going to leave me alone. I asked God to give me patience—now! "God, if you want me to be nice to this guy, I need Your help. I have nothing left to give." Slowing turning to face him, our eyes locked, and then something unexpected happened.

God allowed me to see his humanity. Tension lines marked his forehead and his shoulders drooped. He seemed to be carrying a load of weights. Glancing down, I noticed his over-sized hands. They looked rough and leathery, the marks of a hard laborer. I softened. This man needs a touch of Jesus' love. I threw up another "flash" prayer. "Lord, I've been depending upon myself. I'm too tired to help this guy. Infuse me with Your power." He did.

In that moment of silence, I took another deep breath and then stepped out in faith. Leaning on God's strength, I unraveled a lengthy spiel about the outreach in Peru. My words flowed easily and sincerely. I concluded, "At the end of the drama, the audience will receive an opportunity to either accept Christ as their Savior or reject Him." Looking up into his deep brown eyes, outlined with dark circles, I said, "You have that choice, too."

"Interesting," he muttered thoughtfully.

Whew! I felt like a football player recovering a fumble to score a touchdown. Just like that, in obedience to the Spirit's leading, He gave me strength and changed my attitude.

I inched my way forward, spilled my items on the counter, and paid the cashier. Grabbing my bags, I sauntered outside, my thoughts spinning. The bright sunlight seemed to shed some understanding.

God is not looking for perfect people to save lost souls; He's looking for jars of clay, cracked pots like me, weary and unworthy of holding God's all-surpassing power so that He might be glorified through me. Graham Cooke stated, "He [God] is not seeking a powerful people to represent Him. Rather, He looks for all those who are weak, foolish, despised, and written off, and He inhabits them with His own strength."

I believe God sent this abrasive guy into my life to show me He gives strength to walk the narrow path on the road of difficulty. My competence comes from Him. Only with His energy working in us can we accomplish supernatural things for His glory.

When I get wrapped up in myself, allowing grumpiness and weariness to consume me, it's humanly impossible to reach out. I'd rather ignore people. That's not the way of Jesus; He never gets tired and His compassion never fails.

Whether I'm here in Kansas City, Kansas, caught in a mile-long checkout line, or in Lima, Peru, I will count on God as my source of inexhaustible power. I believe I can do everything through Him who gives me strength.

I climbed in my car and began singing praises to God. I was truly anticipating the mission trip.

Discussion Questions

1. If you were Greg at Wal-Mart, how would you have responded to the antagonistic unbeliever?

2. Oftentimes, outreach is inconvenient; it takes time and energy. In Greg's moment of physical and emotional weakness, what did he do that infused him with fresh inspiration and power?

3. When did Greg's attitude toward this man change?

4. Oswald Chambers says, "If you give of yourself physically, you become exhausted, but if you give of yourself spiritually, you get more strength." Give a personal example of this.

5. How does the above quote reflect the truth in 2 Corinthians 4:7?

"When men see that we are prepared to suffer for the faith we say we hold, they will begin to believe that we really do hold it." —William Barclay

Going the Second Mile

Marty and Sue Vierra as told to Pamela Enderby

"You are to love those who are aliens, for you yourselves were aliens" (Deuteronomy 10:19).

I was exhausted and my nerves frazzled while driving along interstate 40 in a hot, stuffy van. After a long visit with relatives in California, where most people live at a frantic pace, I longed for my quiet, country life in Pauls Valley, Oklahoma.

But God interrupted my plan for rest. A dented station wagon with its hood propped open and two women with small children stood along the road's shoulder waving their arms for help.

When I saw the compassion in my wife's eyes I knew she was thinking my thoughts. "Let's turn around and help those people," I said.

I pulled onto the gravel shoulder and stopped in front of the disabled vehicle. Sue and I climbed out of our van to approach the Native Americans. My heart softened more when I saw loneliness and hopelessness in their eyes.

The old woman, with her arms tightly crossed, met us with a wary smile. Two young, shabbily dressed children clutched the younger woman's legs. We introduced ourselves and offered help. Fortunately, they understood our language well enough and trusted me to begin my investigation of the car's condition.

Peering under the hood, I soon discovered a broken fan belt and suggested we tow their car to the nearest service station. I invited them to wait in our van so they would be protected from the mid-day scorching heat. I retrieved the tow strap buried in my trunk and went to work.

Finally, with the women and children in the back seat of my van and their dilapidated car strapped to my bumper, we inched down the road for three miles until reaching a service station. A young woman was standing behind the counter. When I asked to use her phone book, she shrugged my request and firmly pointed to the pay phone outside.

All the agencies I called turned me down because I was outside their service area. *What should I do now,* I wondered, pushing through the phone booth's doors.

While scanning a stretch of flat prairie, I spotted a salvage yard. With fresh hope, I told the women my plan and we continued our slow journey down the road.

After spending nearly an hour scavenging the junk, we finally discovered a suitable belt and brought it to the proprietor. He shrewdly demanded ten dollars. The helpless strangers shrugged their shoulders and lowered their heads. They had no money. I reached into my billfold, pulled out several bills, and pushed them into his hand.

Driving away from the junkyard I spotted a patrol substation, pulled into its parking lot and explained our dilemma to a police officer. He called two mechanics.

By the time they arrived the sun had set and the evening air had turned chilly. While the women and children huddled together, my wife offered them her jacket. "And here's a blanket," she said. "You may keep it." Her kindness seemed to shock them to silence. Without a word they grabbed the coverings and tightly wrapped their bodies.

After waiting another hour, watching the mechanics fumble with their tools, making progress by trial and error, I instructed them, "Put the car back together as best you can." Then we headed for the mini-mart across the street.

"You must be very hungry. Please take these," Sue said, offering them some sandwiches. Our guests smiled warmly and grabbed the food.

"We are helping you because we want to show you Jesus' love," I explained.

Before our new friends climbed into their repaired car, they turned, smiled, and waved good-bye. Their happy faces rewarded us immensely. We breathed a sigh of relief.

Sometimes it's time-consuming and costly to obey God's call to serve others. When I get self-absorbed, eager to satisfy my own needs, I'm prone to ignore others' needs or use excuses to render myself unusable. With God's help, this time was different.

While traveling home, Sue and I prayed for our new Native American friends and thanked God for allowing us to plant seeds of love into their lives.

Discussion Questions

1. Jesus looked past the prejudices of His day to love the people. Consider how He loved the Samaritan woman in John 4:1-26 and Zacchaeus in Luke 19:2-10. For what reasons did society shun them?

2. Sometimes we neglect the poor and needy. We believe we don't have the time or resources so we expect the government to take responsibility for their wellbeing. How does Jesus' command in John 15:12 speak to this mindset? "Love each other as I have loved you.

Greater love has no man than this that he lay down his life for his friends."

3. As Christ's ambassadors, love for all people should be our standard. What are some common prejudices that hinder you from showing the love of Jesus?

4. "Blessed are the peacemakers, for they will be called sons of God" (Matthew 5:9). Explain Marty and Sue's role as peacemakers.

5. Do you know someone in your community or neighborhood you can reach out to as a form of restitution for past prejudices? Pray Deuteronomy 10:17-19, asking God to help you extend grace to that person.

"Only a few of us will be asked to leave our nets and abandon our professions. The vast majority of Christians will be asked to function within their present occupations, but with a whole new mindset, one that reflects God's perspective on the eternal importance of people." —Bill Hybels

A Doctor Spreads His Infectious Faith

Daniel Hinthorn, M.D. as told to Jeanette Gardner Littleton and Pamela Enderby

"The man who plants and the man who waters have one purpose" (I Corinthians 3:8).

Every time I entered his room, it felt like death. This patient was dying and he knew it. He opened his eyes and announced in a gravelly voice, "Doc, I'm going to die tonight."

Patients have told me that before, and they usually have died, but for some reason this time those words startled me.

Grappling for words, I started talking about God.

"Don't give me that God stuff," the man spat. "I don't want to hear it."

I silently prayed that God would guide me. Then I continued my rounds. Although I'm always open with my faith, I don't talk to everybody. I'm so busy seeing patients, listening to their symptoms and diagnosing their problems, that unless the Holy Spirit prompts me, I usually don't even think about it. But every so often God stops me and says, "Here's someone you need to talk to."

Later, when I returned to his room, he again predicted his demise. "Doc, I'm going to die tonight."

I prayed. "Lord, I don't know what to say. If this man doesn't want to hear about You, I don't have much to offer. Give me the words to say to him."

"Are you ready to die?" I asked.

"No. How do I get ready?"

I told him about sin, about Jesus paying the penalty for it, and about confessing and receiving Jesus as his Savior.

To my surprise, he listened carefully. I could tell he understood my words.

"Would you like to pray?" I finally asked.

"Yeah."

When I turned to close the door to his room, I heard him praying. His words revealed he had a praying mother who loved Jesus and fervently prayed for him throughout his life. He thanked God for her. As he prayed, the sense of death lifted.

I wasn't sure if his praying to receive Christ meant he would be healed, or just that he'd make it to heaven. In fact, I expected to be called during the night to pronounce him dead, but I wasn't. The next morning, I hurried to his room to see how he was doing.

I was stunned. I found the patient sitting up in bed smiling and much improved.

"To everything there is a season, and a time for every matter or purpose under heaven ... a time to plant ... a time to build up ... and a time to pluck up what has been planted. God has made everything beautiful in its time; He has planted eternity in men's heart and mind" (Ecclesiastes 3:1-2, 11 Amp.). Only God knows who and how many others planted and watered seeds of Jesus' love into this man's soul. I just happened to be in the right place at the right time to harvest what was planted, while God ultimately gave the increase.

I'm thankful for this experience because it reminds me to stay alert to people's eternal destiny while attending to their physical needs. I trust the Holy Spirit will continue to interrupt me each time He wants me to share my faith with more sick and dying patients.

Discussion Questions

1. Do you consciously think about the eternal destiny of those you work with? Why or why not?

2. What question(s) might you ask to help determine a person's eternal destiny?

3. Note 1 Corinthians 3:8. What is the role of a watering vessel and a seed bearer? Which one are you most often?

4. As a Spirit-filled believer we can be busy and still take advantage of witnessing opportunities at our workplace, at school, or at home. How is that possible?

5. God plants eternity in people's hearts. If you are willing to heed God's interruptions, what might that require of you?

"Opportunity is missed by most people because it is dressed in overalls and looks like work."
—Thomas Edison

Can Internationals and Christians Be Friends?

Fran Golden as told to Pamela Enderby

"Love never gives up, never loses faith, is always hopeful" (I Corinthians 13:7 TLB).

Teaching English as a second language at a local community college offers unique outreach opportunities to build friendships with immigrants, refugees, and F-1 students (internationals who study in America and then return to their country).

Over the years, I've discovered the most effective way to affect my students is by loving them. That's easier said than done because I'm also rearing two children as a single mom. They require my physical and emotional energy, too. Nevertheless, I carve out time after school to help my students face their fears about living in a new country. That includes helping them overcome language and cultural barriers and creating opportunities to introduce them to Christianity.

My biggest challenge is prioritizing. This year I have twenty students, so everyday I must ask myself hard questions. "Where am I going to spend my minutes and hours?" "How will I give myself and to whom?" King David's prayer for wisdom echoes my heart's cry, "Show me your ways, O Lord, teach me your paths" (Psalm 25:4). I want to show internationals what Jesus can do for people, no matter where they are from or what color skin they have.

Fatima*, a lovely 35-year-old woman, approached me after the 9-11 terrorist attack, crying, "I'm afraid to come to school. And I don't want my children home alone." Television news had spotlighted angry people throwing bottles, shaking their fists, and vandalizing the Muslim elementary school that Fatima's children attended.

In my classroom, suspicious sneers fell upon Fatima and other conservative Muslim women. "I wonder if they had anything to do with the terrorist acts," they whispered. An avalanche of rejection fueled her fear.

I imagined trading places with Fatima. What would it be like living in America, a country that you love, while still feeling loyal to your home country that promotes terrorism? It created a painful tear in my heart for America and also stirred my sympathy for Muslim women.

I warmly encouraged Fatima to stay home. "I'll email your assignments and pray for you. Fear is a terrible thing to live with." Her dark, brown eyes seemed to soften. "Not all Americans blame you," I said. "I know you're a Muslim and I'm a Christian, and of course I think terrorism is a terrible thing. But I don't have anger in my heart toward you, and I don't think you are personally responsible. Some Christians do terrible things, but that doesn't mean I'm guilty for what they have done."

Several weeks later when Fatima returned to school, she thanked me for praying and for trying to understand her needs.

Fear also paralyzed Heba*, a single 25-year-old Muslim woman. She tried hiding her religion by wearing blue jeans and a plain shirt to school. Consequently, other Muslims chided her, threatened to disown her and insisted she at least wear a silk scarf around her head. Unable to handle this peer pressure, she collapsed into an emotional basket case, always crying, and unable to complete her homework. I spent many hours after class comforting Heba with prayer and encouragement.

It seemed best to help Heba get transferred to another ESL program where she felt accepted and safe. No one at her new school forced her to wear a headscarf and be labeled Muslim; however, loneliness remained her companion. She greatly missed a few close Muslim friends she had left behind.

Every week after that, Heba quietly slipped into my office, risking harsh criticisms, in order to show her appreciation. Presenting me with a gift or note, she'd say, "Thank you for helping me through this hard time. You're a wonderful friend. You were the only one I could talk to when I was afraid."

Our language barrier had to be overcome in order to become friends. Many internationals live in our country for one, two, or three years without ever speaking to an American. Why? Asians are typically shy; they cluster together with people from their own country. Likewise, Americans admit trying to understand internationals is just too much effort.

So, I'm purposefully adhering to the Apostle Paul's words: "As God's chosen people, holy and dearly loved, clothe yourselves with compassion, kindness, humility, gentleness, and patience" (Colossians 3:12). After school, at break, and sometimes during class, I take my students aside individually and ask personal questions like, "Is your family here or still in your country?" "Do you live alone?" "Do you have a husband or children?" As I listen to their fragmented explanations in an informal setting, their English conversational skills improve. Also, addressing internationals by their native foreign names with correct pronunciation reflects respect and honor, a sure way to nurture friendship. Interestingly, I learned that when my students feel respected and cared for, their learning ability increases by two or three times.

Cultural differences can create a nightmarish experience or a memorable one. Within the first few months of living in America, an international will either fail or succeed. For that reason, I'm intentional about outreach. Philippians 2:4 commands, "Each of you should look not only to your own interests, but also to the interests of others." Foreigners need transportation to their jobs, schools, or shopping. They need to understand the legal mumbo-jumbo of rental contracts before signing an agreement. They need furniture such as chairs, tables, small appliances, and kitchen utensils.

Loneliness is also their constant companion. I invite internationals to my house for family cookouts, recreational activities, and holiday festivities. I cultivate their friendship, and they're more likely to listen to me when I introduce them to Christianity.

Sharing my faith in school happens quite naturally when I weave basic Christian truths into my curriculum. Before my students undertake the assignment of explaining their native country's marriage customs, food, and holidays, I model the assignment with a Christian viewpoint. Take Easter, for example. "It's the season when life is full of rebirth," I explain and then point them to 1 Corinthians 15:3. "Christ died for our sins according to the Scriptures. He was buried, and he was raised on the third day." With their curiosity aroused, more conversation flows. "Salvation is found in no one else, for there is no other name under heaven given to man by which we must be saved" (Acts 4:12). I never put pressure on them to accept my beliefs. I simply tell them, "I know you may not believe this, but I think it's still good for you to understand Christianity."

I heard someone say, "More is caught than taught." If we live self-controlled, upright, and godly lives, I think internationals will experience spiritual awakenings. Genden*, a refugee and former Buddhist priest from Tibet, confirmed this truth. In 1956, when Tibetans rioted against communism, Buddhist priests were lined up and shot down with machine guns in the temple. At age 15, Genden fled on foot, climbed the Himalaya Mountains, and settled in India with the Dalai Lama and other Buddhist priests. For the next five years, Genden lived in a refugee camp and sat under the teachings of the Dalai Lama.

The Dalai Lama is the chief pontiff and government ruler of Tibet and a highly respected spiritual leader. Tibetans regard the Dalai as Buddha reincarnated.

After one semester, before leaving class one afternoon, Genden remarked, "In all my life, the most special thing I've done is sit under the Dalai Lama. But, being in your classroom I felt something I've never felt from the Dalai Lama. You really care for each person, and you help each person with his or her needs. I can't say the Dalai Lama ever made me feel that way."

Immediately, I recognized the witnessing opportunity, and I used his beautiful compliment to turn his eyes toward the one, true God. I replied, "The reason I am who I am is because God gives me the ability to show compassion and love. Being a Christian is more than being a kind person. It's letting the life of God flow from me. God is who you see in me; that's who you want!"

From that time on, I gently encouraged Genden, "Cry out to God and you will find Him. Don't give up your search. The Word of God promises, 'Those who seek Me find Me' (Proverbs 8:17). I believe God is God, no matter what country you're from or what religion you believe in. If your heart really wants to know the true God, He will reveal Himself to you. I can't do it, but I know my God can. He is faithful." Somewhere throughout the course of life, I think God will reveal Himself to Genden because he has a true cry in his heart for God.

Frequently, I take my class roster, call out their names to the Lord, and pray, "Would You touch them and use me to love them while they're here?" I believe prayer accomplishes things that nothing else can.

John Knox, 16th century religious reformer, stated, "When I think of those who have influenced my life the most, I think not of the great but of the good." I agree. It doesn't take a super spiritual Christian to build friendships with internationals. It simply takes willingness to love them God's way.

*Names changed.

Discussion Questions

1. How did Fran love her students God's way?

2. Imagine living in another country. What difficulties might you face? How could you help internationals overcome these difficulties in America, thereby building bridges with them?

3. "You will never find time for anything. If you want time, you must make it," stated Charles Buxton. Fran stated that as a single mom and full time teacher her biggest challenge is "taking time to love people." What questions does she frequently ask herself to help prioritize her time? Why is it necessary to establish daily goals for building relationships?

4. What specific ways did Fran bridge friendships with her international students that we could imitate?

5. If you invited an international to your home for Christmas or Easter, how would you weave Christian truths into your celebration?

Focus first on God himself. As you tell your world of Christ, you'll find He'll meet your need! —Jill Briscoe

Kool-Aid, Kids, and Christ

Kay Rice as told to Pamela Enderby

"His divine power has given us everything we need for life and godliness" (1 Peter 1:3).

When my kids pleaded with me to have a backyard Bible club, I considered the idea and then focused on my inabilities: I always seemed to be short on time, I wasn't familiar with children's Bible curricula, and I was too tired to undertake a huge project. To be honest, I also cringed at the thought of cluttering my brand new dining room table with craft supplies!

On the positive side, I considered my son Nathan's salvation. He had come to Christ while attending a backyard Bible club a couple of years earlier, and I realized that's where my other kids' spiritual lives blossomed. I also realized that inviting my neighborhood kids to my home instead of my church would seem less threatening.

With my four kids' strong nudges and their promises to pitch in, I put my faith and my feet to work. Here's how I proceeded:

I decided whom to invite. I targeted four through twelve-year olds, in keeping with the ages of my kids. I used the older children as "helpers."

I chose a date and time. I chose early August because summer sports usually have ended and parents are looking for ways to entertain their bored kids. I started at 10:00 a.m. taking into consideration relaxed summer schedules and ended at 11:30 a.m., Monday through Friday.

I chose a theme. After evaluating a plethora of resources at the Christian bookstore, I chose a medieval theme from Gospel Light. Their materials offer exciting theme-based craft ideas and catchy songs. I also used Child Evangelism's Wordless book, which uses colored pages to place a heavy emphasis on salvation through Christ's work on the cross. The children received solid, Biblical teaching enhanced by entertaining activities.

I designed a flyer. Using my modest computer skills, I was able to produce a colorful, eye-catching flyer complete with a castle design. I included the four Ws: Who, What, When, Where, and an RSVP. To encourage parental involvement, I invited parents to attend and requested specific craft items from them. This put the parents at ease and did away with the uncomfortable feeling of "getting something for nothing." My bold 13-year-old delivered the invitations to each neighbor two weeks before the event, and I mailed a few to my kids' school friends.

I developed a format. The preliminaries for each day included warm greetings, issuing nametags, and announcements. Then we sang songs, including our theme song. We practiced the same Bible verse each day (to ensure they'd learn it), listened to a Bible story, and ended with crafts, games, and snacks (often provided by other parents).

I celebrated with the children and parents. On the final day, we put on a short program for the parents. A processional song played while the children paraded in wearing simple costumes they created at home fashioned after our medieval theme. The children recited their Bible verse simultaneously, sang their theme song and explained each color of the Wordless Book. I displayed the kid's crafts: a coat of arms and castle garden stepping-stones. The "royal feast" followed. I provided barbecued chicken wings and other parents brought finger foods.

To my surprise, I thoroughly enjoyed this outreach. One day, during story time, I showed a picture depicting a cross that bridged the gap between heaven and earth. Six-year old Anna's eyes lit up and she exclaimed, "That's a cool picture!" The children's eagerness to hear the Truth kept them attentive all week and fueled my enthusiasm. Never did they complain, "I heard this before."

One day, an unchurched mom offered to help. I gulped. It happened to be the day for teaching the Biblical view of creation, how sin entered the world and its effect on us. I prayed for courage to teach the lesson truthfully and boldly. Although she didn't receive salvation, she heard the Word of God that promises never to return void. Later, I received her note thanking me for my positive influence on her son. "Every day he sings the Bible songs you taught him."

Throughout the week, children responded to the Truth after each lesson. Three children made decisions for Christ, one received reassurance for her salvation, and another needed comfort and prayer while grieving her friend's illness.

Before I delved into this outreach, I thought sharing the Gospel would be difficult. But God gave me all I needed: wisdom, strength, and courage to reach hungry souls in my own backyard.

Discussion Questions

1. Often the thought of reaching out to our neighbors seems overwhelming because we focus on our weaknesses. Read Matthew 14:15-21. What dilemma did the disciples face?

2. How did Jesus alleviate their problem?

3. When you feel the odds stacked against you, consider 1 Peter 1:3. What promise does it offer you?

4. The minute we take one step of obedience, God opens up opportunities to show His glory through us. In what ways did God show His glory through Kay?

5. Do you need spiritual vision for a seemingly impossible outreach in your neighborhood or community? Ask God to give you courage to take the first step of obedience. Now move ahead in faith by making a practical, step-by-step plan.

The great use of life is to spend it for something that outlasts it. —William James

Navigating Fourth Graders for God

Vicki Lipira as told to Pamela Enderby

"Teach us to number our days aright, that we may gain a heart of wisdom" (Psalm 90:12).

"I think kids are better off not going to church! Too many kids grow up in the church and then become rebellious teenagers. Too much religion turns them off."

This stinging remark by my unchurched friend rattled me because she was partially right. I had seen dozens of dismayed parents lamenting over their wayward teens who once demonstrated a genuine faith in Jesus Christ.

I defended my daughter's Christian training. "Brandi started attending Sunday school as a pre-schooler. She learned songs about Jesus and she still loves to sing them. Hearing Bible stories about God's creation and His miracles are laying the foundation for her faith. Brandi's entering fourth grade now, and she's begging me to lead an after-school Bible study for her classmates and neighborhood friends. She wants them to know Jesus too!"

"Just wait and you'll see," she murmured in an arrogant tone and backed off.

Watch my 9-year-old grow up into a rebellious teen? I entertained that possibility. Suddenly, I felt uneasy and threatened by this huge responsibility to help navigate Brandi's spiritual journey. Should I support Brandi's desire to evangelize her classmates, or should I encourage her to lighten up on her spiritual ambitions?

After prayerfully considering my options, I wasn't convinced all teens had turned rebellious because they got "too much religion" as kids. When Jesus assigned the Great Commission, He put a high priority on children. Jesus even used children as examples to show how we must come to the Father. "Let the little children come to me, and do not hinder them, for the kingdom of heaven belongs to such as these" (Matthew 19:14).

I was also moved by Barna's alarming report. "Of the 51 million children under the age of 18 in the United States, more than 40 million do not know Jesus Christ as their Savior."

I determined to dig in my heels, ignore my friend's pessimism, and support Brandi's spiritual quest. In doing so, it stretched my faith. Adding a kids' Bible study to my already busy schedule, I had to lean hard on God's wisdom, strength, and understanding like never before. I also came to realize the urgency of sowing God's Word in children's lives.

William Carey, a courageous Baptist missionary to India, once said, "Expect great things from God and attempt great things for God." With high aspirations, I endeavored to help fourth graders cultivate their relationship with God. Consequently, He unfolded some great plans.

"O.K., Brandi, I'll lead this Bible study," I said, "But only if you help me." Involving Brandi gave her ownership of the Bible study and practice in exercising outreach boldness. We often prayed together for the girls to have receptive hearts; then Brandi extended personal invitations to her friends at recess and after school. I followed up with phone calls to parents. (Room mothering at Brandi's school for several years earlier had earned me their trust.) I shared details, including the starting date, meeting times, and the Bible study's purpose. "I think this Bible study will help our girls grow deeper, more meaningful friendships, and it will give them a better understanding about who God is and how to know Him better."

For several weeks after school, ten little girls gathered in my living room to learn about Jesus. At times, I felt a little overwhelmed juggling family, church, and school responsibilities, so I'd have to put my perfectionist tendencies to flight and succumb to taking short cuts. Hungry kids enjoy store bought snacks as much as home-made ones and offering recycled spiritual truths affect kids as much as fresh spiritual discoveries. I served the girls spiritual truths I had gleaned from my weekly women's Bible study or my daily Bible reading. Scriptures pertinent to jealousy, self-esteem, and gossip created lively discussions. For example, the Bible reveals the damage of gossip (Proverbs 11:13, 16:28, 18:6-8) and its consequences (Psalm 101:5 and Proverbs 8:13).

I discovered that kids' Bible lessons don't require dozens of preparation hours. The Bible packs a punch. It's "living and active … it judges the thoughts and attitudes of the heart" (Hebrews 4:12).

I grew excited watching the girls grab hold of God's Word. As their knowledge of God increased, so did their faith and willingness to share personal concerns with each other. Lifting one another up to the Lord, offering simple, yet heartfelt prayers, knit their hearts together. With time, their answered prayers helped expand their prayer focus to include the needs of outside friends and family members, including Mrs. Evans, their unsaved teacher.

"Let's do a drama that will present the Gospel to Mrs. Evans," I suggested. The girls' enthusiasm inspired me to write a simple script. After several weeks of practicing, Mrs. Evans accepted the girls' invitation to their homespun drama.

I narrated while each girl, donned in a Burger King crown and a sign hanging from her neck, took turns sitting on a throne (a decorated chair). Each sign identified an object or person promising happiness, such as toys, bicycles, friends, computer games, parents, and movies.

As I explained how those things failed to fulfill each girls' need for inner peace and happiness, the girls' faces drooped with sadness. Finally, one of the unhappy little girls was invited to church. (She exited the room.) After learning about Jesus and receiving Him as Savior, she put Him on the throne of her life. (She cheerfully returned, no longer wearing the king's hat and sign.) Her short testimony concluded the play by sharing how she accepted Jesus into her heart and how it brought her true happiness.

Mrs. Evans listened intently. After enjoying the drama and refreshments she thanked us in her usual charming way and left. Mrs. Evans didn't receive the gift of salvation that day, but this economical, fun-filled outreach definitely stimulated our evangelistic desires. We began to pray more for the unsaved and we brainstormed more outreach ideas. Cultivating an outreach mindset added fresh purpose to our meetings.

About seven years later, when Brandi entered her mid-teen years, she rebelled. During those tumultuous years I questioned the faithfulness of God. I could hear my friend's callous comment mocking my faith, "Just wait and see."

Hurt and disappointed, I still chose to cling to the truth. "Train up a child in the way he should go, and when he is old he will not turn from it" (Proverbs 22:6). As a young child Brandi had received a lot of spiritual seeds in her tender heart. I believed that God's Word and His promises would never return void. So I stood on the authority of His

Word and claimed a promised victory for Brandi even while there were no signs of victory.

When Brandi reached her twenties, she turned back to God, and today she enjoys a flourishing relationship with Him. The seeds sown in her heart throughout her youth, especially during the girls' Bible study, surely blossomed.

Another priceless reward I received from leading this fourth grader's Bible study came one morning when I received news that Anneta and Carla, two girls who had attended the Bible study, had been killed in a car accident. Losing them saddened me; however, I experienced peace. I could remember the afternoon at Bible study when they prayed to receive Christ into their hearts. Today I imagine Anneta and Carla resting safely in Jesus' arms.

Such tragedies remind me of the urgency to sow God's Word into lost souls. Too often I'm apathetic or consumed with self-interests. But tragedies are no respecters of persons. They wait for no one.

I'm thankful I didn't dismiss Brandi's plea to help her share her faith. It's what truly makes my life rich and fulfilling. And who knows when eternity will come knocking on the door of children's lives?

Discussion Questions

1. How would you respond to the comment, "I think kids are better off not going to church."

2. According to George Barna Research Group findings, children between the ages of 5 and 13 have a 32 percent probability of accepting Jesus as their Savior; children between the ages of 14 and 18 have a 4 percent chance; those older than 18 have a 6 percent chance. Why do you think the percentage decreases with age?

3. Perhaps leading a children's Bible study is not for you. What other ways can you influence children for Christ?

4. Have you shared Christ with someone and then discovered his or her life was taken unexpectedly by a tragedy? Take a moment to pray through Psalm 90:12.

~

Obstacle Three: I Like Staying In My Comfort Zone.

"Thanks be to God, who always leads us in trium-
phal procession in Christ and through us spreads
everywhere the fragrance of the knowledge of Him"

(2 Corinthians 2:14).

Too many Christians are no longer fishers of men but keepers of the aquarium. —*Paul Harvey*

My Crazy Knitting Club and What They Taught Me

Beth Severson as told to Pamela Enderby

"I have become all things to all men, so that by all possible means I might save some" (I Corinthians 9:22).

Our evangelism pastor bellowed, "Don't hang out at the club! Get some non-Christian friends. It's so easy for people in big churches to hang out at the club with their Christian friends doing Christian things. We need to be kicked out!"

His challenge hit me hard because I was guilty. After living in the same suburban community for seventeen years and attending the same big church, my social life outside the church had grown stagnant. Church activities kept me tied to my Christian friends and family. Hanging out with the same crowd put a tight lid on possibilities for sharing my faith.

After our family moved from Wisconsin to Kansas and settled into our new home, I decided to make a fresh start.

"Lord, I want to get involved with some non-Christians. How do I make friends with them? Where do I go?" It didn't take long before God answered that prayer. He cracked open the door of my spiritually stuffy world and directed me outside to women needing a Savior.

At my kids' school, I heard about a knitting group that included elementary, middle school and high-school moms. *Hmmm ... knitting. I vaguely remember how to do that, I* thought. After expressing minimal interest, I received weekly voice mails encouraging my attendance. Although I sensed the Lord presenting this opportunity, I hesitated to go for two reasons. First, I presumed mothers whose kids are a lot older or younger than mine might be difficult to connect with. Second, I vaguely remembered how to knit. How could I comfortably fit in with a bunch of serious knitters? After a few more phone invitations, I put my hesitations aside. I'll give the "Knit-Whit" club a whirl at least once.

I expected to meet some serious knitters, women wielding knitting needles with expensive yarn destined for elaborate lace scarves or warm, fuzzy sweaters. These ladies hardly met my expectations. Most weeks they set knitting aside for shopping trips and lunch at ritzy restaurants. Other afternoons we did scrap booking, beading, and painting ceramic plates. One Valentine's Day marks the most memorable event for me. This charming party, with cake and coffee, featured our weddings. We giggled through the afternoon, sharing outdated wedding pictures and reminiscing the drama of being newly wed.

Of course, I also faced uncomfortable times with my non-Christian friends. To be exact, at times I felt more like an alien from another planet. Clashing convictions about moral, family, and political values made me squirm. My insides twisted and turned when colorful gab about reality TV shows such as The Bachelorette dominated the conversation.

Although I sometimes felt trapped in this spiritually toxic climate and considered quitting the club, I tried to refocus on the wonderful opportunities I had experienced with the younger mothers. The very thing I had feared, our wide age differences, turned out to foster meaningful conversations. They looked to me for advice about parenting. Being the "older mom" in the group allowed God to speak through me to offer mothers hope, encouragement, and comfort through their pangs and challenges. I prayed to be an attractive vessel, one that would draw and stir their hearts toward God.

After five months of socializing with my Knit-Whit girlfriends, I took the next step. "Let's start a neighborhood Bible study," I encouraged Shelly, my Christian friend. "You can invite your unchurched friends as well." Shelly had never been involved in such an outreach, but I rallied her support anyway, and she helped me get the idea rolling.

We were nervous about possibly losing the relationships we had carefully nurtured. Yet, we believed God was prompting us to get started.

One evening Shelly stopped by my house with the Bible study invitations we planned to hand deliver. "I'm totally out of my comfort zone," she laughed nervously. I, too, began wrestling with negative thoughts. *What will people in the group think about me? Will this hinder my friendships with them?*

"Shelly, maybe we shouldn't do it right now; maybe we should do it another time." I wanted to give Shelly a way out.

"No," she replied. "I know God wants me to do this." Her firm response fueled my desire and assured me that God had called us to this Bible study.

Shelly and I chose a book called *The Lenten Bible Study*. Our prospect list included women representing different church backgrounds and denominations, some not practicing their faith at all. We figured we'd find common ground around the season of Lent because most of us do something for Lent.

The next day, on the way to meeting my Knit-Whit girl-friends for lunch, my thoughts lingered on past social events where friendships were bridged. We enjoyed so many crazy, fun times together. Now, I was about to invite them to Bible study!

Walking into this scary yet exciting situation reminded me of Bill Hybel's advice in *The Contagious Christian* to invite the lost to a Bible study or church event after first having "bar-be-cue." In other words, enjoy outside activities with your non-Christian friends in a relaxed, non-threatening environment first. That will help create favorable attitudes toward your invitations to church activities later. I had done that.

Now, excitement and apprehension bubbled in my heart and thrust me forward. I prayed, "Lord, if you want me to invite these women to this Bible study I know You'll work it out. Prompt me in my spirit, 'This is the time; these are the women.'"

Several of us sat and chatted till mid-afternoon, and then some women began to head for home, leaving five women sitting around the kitchen table, eating dessert. Interestingly, I had developed the strongest relationships with those particular five, being room moms, through our book club, through our children's soccer and basketball games, and through our crazy knitting group that frequently socializes but seldom knits.

Suddenly, everyone grew quiet. *Oh, this is the opportunity,* I thought. Swallowing hard, I nervously pulled out my invitations and plopped them on the table.

"You know, guys, I was thinking, wouldn't it be fun to have a Bible study for the six weeks of Lent. Just among us neighbors. We wouldn't promote or talk about any of our churches, we would just study the season of Lent, the Lord Jesus, and the Scriptures." Silence. More silence. The longer it lingered, the more knots tied my stomach. I silently pleaded, "Lord Jesus, salvage this, please!"

Finally, one of the girls picked up an invitation. Turning it over and studying it, she enthusiastically said, "I think this is a really neat idea." After the others asked questions, they, too, seemed eager to participate. By the time I left, four of the five women told me to count them in and eventually the fifth one came along too. Shelly had a similar experience with her friends.

Shelly and I met regularly to pray for the Bible study. Many of our friends would be new to one another for their children attended five different area schools. We specifically asked God to encourage the women to enjoy each other and to create a hunger within each woman to know Him.

The Bible study met in each other's homes, which cultivated commitment, and I also challenged the women to take turns leading the study. "We're all learning together," I said. "Experts are just people asking the questions, so we're all experts!"

At the conclusion of our six-week study, one lady asked if the group could continue. She enjoyed learning about the Bible and she especially enjoyed the comments from "the more learned women in the group." Amazingly, everyone shared similar sentiments and agreed to continue. I, too, experienced peace and assurance that I was doing exactly what God wanted me to be doing.

God answered Shelly's and my prayers. We found that He truly is "able to do immeasurably more than all we ask or imagine, according to His power that is at work within us" (Ephesians 3:20). After getting into the second week of our second study titled "They Met Jesus," I received an incredible card in the mail from one of the women.

"I just want to thank you from the bottom of my heart for inviting me to Bible study. It has meant more to me than you will ever imagine. I'm not sure I can put into words what it has done for me.

"I never before understood what it meant to ask Jesus to come into your heart, but now I do. I have, and I know He is now there. It was such a simple thing to do, but it has made such a powerful, meaningful effect on me. It was more than I ever expected. Not only has the Lord given me a gift of faith and belief, I believe He has given you one also. If it weren't for you (and the ladies of the group), I would not have come to Him. Again, thank you and God bless you."

Shortly after receiving Sue's* card, I invited her to meet with me for coffee. Sipping a cup of café mocha at Starbuck's, listening to Sue share her new found spiritual insights made my day! Her eyes welled up with tears. While trying to hide her embarrassment, I said, "When we realize what Christ has done for us, how much He loves us, and how much we're forgiven, it's natural to experience tears."

God has His finger on the pulse of our Bible study. I'm amazed at how sensitive and actively He's drawing women to Himself, and I'm learning that their spiritual journey doesn't have to mirror mine. The Holy Spirit will change them His way and in His time.

Discussion Questions

1. What are the advantages of having a "bar-be-cue" with your unsaved friends before inviting them to a church event?

2. List some of the things Beth and Shelly did to help their outreach Bible study become a success?

3. How did Beth and Shelly overcome their fears?

4. Beth lived out I Corinthians 9:22. She worked at "becoming all things to all [wo]men." If you are willing to do the same, what risks might this require of you?

Tell me whom you love and I will tell you
who you are. —Houssaye

Putting Away Pride

Pamela Enderby

"My brothers, as believers in our glorious Lord Jesus
Christ, don't show favoritism" (James 2:1).

Entering ten years of teaching my kids at home, I battled a malady common to most home-schooling moms. I
call it "Cinderella-itis." While instructing math, reading,
science, and spelling, in addition to house cleaning, preparing meals and doing laundry, I grew weary and felt unap-
preciated. Then I received an invitation to lead a weekly
Bible study for a group of prestigious women. I eagerly accepted the opportunity.

I enjoyed listening and watching these young believers
grow in prayer and Bible knowledge and genuinely cared
about their spiritual growth.

One morning at Bible study after the ladies shared their
prayer requests, a hacking cough arrested my attention. I
looked up and spotted Bill, the maintenance man across the
room, changing light bulbs. My eyes fixed on his faded
blue jeans and wrinkled plaid shirt. Immediately I judged

him. He should be dressed more appropriately in a place like this. Then just before Bill left the room, his blue eyes locked with mine, and unexpectedly, their emptiness pierced my heart. For that moment I saw beyond his appearance. I bowed my head and closed my eyes to pray with the ladies. Tears began to fill my eyes, and it seemed for a long time I couldn't speak.

"Ladies," I finally stammered, half embarrassed, "I believe God is leading us to pray for Bill this morning." What might they think of me, asking them to spend time in prayer for this man?

Choking back more tears, I swallowed hard and prayed, "God, would You please touch Bill's life today. He needs You."

That simple prayer, stirred by the work of the Holy Spirit, launched a chain of events and began to accomplish God's greater purposes. Ironically, God was about to use me to help Bill find Jesus. First, He had to change me.

Driving home from Bible study that day, God began gently convicting me of my arrogant attitude. All those weeks, I had disregarded Bill's lostness for my personal interests.

Then the enemy accused me. "Who do you think you are? If those ladies could really see what's in your heart, they wouldn't think so highly of you."

By the time I arrived home I had decided to turn the study over to someone else. I knelt down in my bedroom and told God I was willing to step away from teaching the Bible study. But the One who forgives encouraged me to keep going.

The following Thursday I returned to Bible study with a transformed heart and a desire to reach out to Bill. Serving Bill became my ambition and consequently fueled ongoing prayer for him at Bible study. God also put me on a path of kind deeds. When I baked fresh bread and cookies for my family, Bill received his fair share coupled with occasional encouraging notes.

Some mornings I arrived early to spend time chatting with Bill. My kind deeds grew tiny seeds of trust in Bill's heart. When he began sharing his broken dreams, sorrows, and hopes, I was thrilled.

One spring morning when I arrived early for Bible study to give Bill a plate of goodies, he was missing. I searched for him outside in his usual gardening spot. He wasn't there. I checked the dining room. Not there. I looked in the fitness center. Not there. Finally, after roaming throughout the clubhouse, I found Bill in the kitchen pantry, gathering cleaning supplies.

"I've been looking all over for you. Why aren't you gardening?"

He muttered something about feeling weak and dizzy. I felt a nudge to pray for him.

"Bill," I said, gently. "Would you like me to pray for you?"

"Yes," he whispered.

After praying for Bill's health, prompted by the Holy Spirit, I asked a bold question. "Bill, do you have a personal relationship with Jesus?" I spotted that hollow look in his eyes again and explained God's plan of salvation. Bill listened carefully.

"Bill, "I continued, calmly. "You can receive eternal life, too. Would you like to pray to receive Jesus?"

"I don't know how to pray," he said.

"If I pray would you like to repeat the words after me?"

Bill nodded.

Reaching out to him, I placed my hand on his shoulder and prayed words from my heart that I thought expressed Bill's need for Jesus and his desire to put his trust in Him. With his head bowed, tears trickled down his cheeks.

When I finished, Bill looked up, his eyes softened. Undoubtedly, my simple yet sincere prayer moved God to create a divine exchange: Bill's earthly rags for the beautiful garment of salvation.

The following week I offered Bill an NIV study Bible and some literature on how to grow his new life in Christ. Bill eagerly received all of it.

A few months later Bill unexpectedly passed away. Yes, he failed to achieve all the earthly goals and dreams he had shared with me, but I'm certain he entered eternity full of peace and joy.

"Has not God chosen those who are poor in the eyes of the world to be rich in faith and to inherit the kingdom he promised those who love him? (James 2:5). Leading the less fortunate and lonely to the throne of grace is one of the greatest privileges anyone can experience.

Loving God and loving the unlovely without judging them go hand in hand. Neither is really complete without the other.

Discussion Questions

1. Arrogant attitudes keep us from viewing others from God's standards. They display themselves by being more interested in enjoying the acceptance of peers. What is God's standard? Consider Philippians 2:3.

2. Someone once defined humility as having a teachable spirit. What is your definition of humility?

3. Why is humility needed in order to step out of your comfort zone?

4. Who might be drawn closer to Christ if you exercised humility? Prayerfully consider how you can begin to demonstrate humility toward that person. What might that require of you?

Some wish to live within the sound of church bells; I
want to run a rescue shop within a yard of hell.
—*C. T. Studd*

No Parking
Evangelism

Glenda Ingram as told to Dorothy Klass and Pamela Enderby

"Go to the street corners and invite to the banquet anyone
you can find"(Matthew 22: 9).

There it was again, that voice I knew so well. The idea
of witnessing in unfamiliar territory burned in me.

The first time I heard it was an early Sunday morning
while driving to church where I taught a young adult Sunday school class. As I went around a curve, I saw men and
boys playing basketball, polishing cars, and just hanging
out.

At first, I thought our young adult class could witness
to this crowd of men. I was teaching a series on soul winning and this would be a good opportunity for the class to
have hands-on-experience. When I told my pastor about my
idea, he said we couldn't take the class away from the
church. I didn't push my idea, but it lingered in my mind.

Eight years later, on a beautiful Sunday morning, God spoke a little louder as I went around that same curve. "Now it's time to minister to these men." The guys who were playing basketball appeared to be the same men I had seen Sunday after Sunday.

By that time, I was attending a different church and was enrolled in the new members' class; I had two more sessions left. I prayed, "Lord, if You will give me the grace to attend the last two classes, after that I will stop and talk to these men."

I will never forget the first Sunday morning when I "spied out the land." I was apprehensive, of course, because I didn't know whether I would be received or rejected. I did not appear to have anything in common with these men. They were athletic, physically fit, and energized. I am a grandma and not physically fit! I definitely don't fit in with a bunch of jocks!

That morning I was pressed in my spirit to ask the men three questions. "Are you playing for a league," or "Are you Seventh Day Adventists?" If they answered "yes" to either of these questions, I would know why they continued to play on Sundays. They answered "no" both times.

The third question was the hardest. "May I come and pray for you every week and share God's Word for about 15 or 20 minutes?" Because of a ruptured disc in my back, I couldn't stand any longer than that.

Two of the men were especially friendly and immediately introduced me to the others. I had planned to stop for only a few minutes to line everything up, but as men approached me individually, requesting prayer, I stayed for two hours.

I was physically exhausted yet spiritually energized when I left. God was confirming my efforts. As I drove away, I remember questioning God, "Why did I have to ask for their permission to speak to them? This is a public park; anybody can come here."

He answered, "If you had not asked, you would have trespassed against their will, and they would have resisted Me." I learned from that initial experience to always seek God for the messages I would give them.

The next Sunday He gave me the message titled "God's Gift." It was burning within me. As I entered the park, a hand-printed sign on a tree said "John 3:16." This Scripture confirmed God's desire that I speak about His gift to mankind.

As soon as the men saw me drive into the parking lot, they surrounded me. I remember asking if anyone had ever bought a gift for someone only to have it rejected. I pointed out how much more God must hurt when we reject His only Son, His gift of salvation. "It's a slap in God's face," I said.

Their thoughtful expressions revealed that God had their attention. We stood in a circle as I walked around praying a special prayer for each one. Two of the men gave their lives to the Lord that day!

The next week the guys reported that one of their buddies had suffered a heat stroke and convulsions and was taken to the emergency room. He was one I had laid hands on the week before. The nurse said he was lucky to be alive, but the guys credited my prayer for saving his life. "We know God sent you here," they said.

Every Sunday I looked forward to being with my new friends. Some of the rough ones were on drugs or dealing drugs. Others were there just to have a good time, but they all needed Jesus. Some Sundays, instead of sharing God's Word, I would just pray with them and leave. But I went faithfully Sunday after Sunday.

Several months later, the Lord did a wonderful thing. I had complained that only two men had confessed salvation. "Why hasn't anyone else been saved?"

God seemed to impress the following message upon my heart: "Talk about salvation and make it simple."

The following Sunday, I couldn't seem to get a message from the Lord and for the first time, unlike the other times, I actually dreaded going. A couple of men eagerly greeted me at the court when I arrived about five minutes late. "Pastor, we're ready for the Word this morning."

Stalling for a few more minutes, hoping God would speak to me, I said, "You finish your game and then we'll have service." I felt empty.

Just minutes before their game ended, one of the guys running up the court caught my eye. When I noticed a tattoo on his arm, immediately Isaiah 49:15-16a came into my mind. "Can a mother forget the baby at her breast and have no compassion on the child she has borne? Though she may forget, I will not forget you! See, I have engraved (tattooed) you on the palms of my hands."

For the next five minutes I felt as if I were on fire with God's message. I talked about a good mama and a troubled (bad) mama. A bad mama might forget the son of her womb, but God said He would never forget us. He said He has tattooed a picture of us on His hands. Our faces are ever before Him.

"The Bible says that if you believe in your heart and confess with your mouth, you will be saved. How many of you believe in your heart that Jesus is the Son of God?"

A few men responded, "I believe! I believe!"

"Do you believe that he died on the Cross? Do you believe He rose from the dead?" I thundered.

They shouted, "I believe! I believe!"

"Then if you believe in your heart, open your mouth, and tell the other men!" They jumped to their feet, proclaiming Jesus' name!

That morning 29 men gave their hearts to the Lord! The guy with the tattoo also gave his life to Jesus along with his five-year-old daughter. God affirmed me. "You made the message so simple that even a five-year-old could understand."

Later that day as I thought about the amazing way God had worked, He spoke to me again. "How long has it been since you've been ministering to these men?"

"Well, Lord, it's been nine months."

He said, "You gave birth today."

After that Sunday, the men started bringing Bibles in their athletic bags. Now sharing God's Word lasts 45 minutes to an hour and nobody pays attention to time.

After service one Sunday, a distraught father introduced me to his two teenage daughters and two nieces. Since teenagers love to eat, I treated them to breakfast. "Who wants to say grace?" I asked, as they delved into their food. One of the nieces recited, "God is great. God is good. Thank you for this food. Amen." They probably thought I was finished with the religious stuff, but I kept the conversation going. "Girls," I said, "How do you talk to God? How do you pray?"

One girl quoted, "Now I lay me down to sleep, I pray the Lord my soul to keep." Hearing these teens recite form prayers implied they lacked a personal relationship with Jesus. Before we left the restaurant, I shared the Good News, and over time, all of them gave their hearts to the Lord.

When I began this ministry God promised, "When you see change in these men, you'll see change in this community." He was right! These guys are becoming good fathers, good husbands, good friends, good community leaders, and good brothers! Even their family members are receiving salvation!

What God has done in nine months with these men (and with me) as we huddle together on the basketball court and study His Word exceeds my wildest expectations. I had no idea, when I was just driving by on the way to church one morning, what God had planned for these men. He was patiently waiting on me to get started.

Discussion Questions

1. God's timing to fulfill His plans is perfect. Glenda waited eight years before she "got started" sharing her faith at the park. God sometimes causes us to wait. Why? What do you think might have been accomplished by waiting?

2. What personal obstacles could have caused Glenda to stay in her comfort zone? What personal obstacles could be keeping you from relating to some(one) outside your comfort zone?

3. Showing the men courtesy and respect was a key factor in winning their favor. How do you show courtesy and respect to unbelievers God has placed in your life?

4. The man's tattoo and the girl's prayer at lunch became springboards for outreach conversation. Recall a recent conversation or something you saw that might have been a bridge for outreach conversation. In other words, how could you have brought God into the situation?

5. Today, if you were given the opportunity to share John 3:16, "For God so loved the world that He gave His only begotten Son, that whoever believes in Him should not perish but have everlasting life," how would you keep it simple?

If we really wish to help and to save men, our attitude
must not be that of condemnation but that of
pleading; our accent must not be that of criticism but
of compassion. —William Barclay

My Porn Story

Debbie Simpson as told to Pamela Enderby

"A word aptly spoken is like apples of gold in settings of
silver" (Proverbs 25:11).

As I approached the computer workstation at the public
library, I suddenly felt uneasy. Glancing down at one of the
screens, I gasped. "What was that?"

One after another, sordid pornographic pictures appeared. A teenage boy donned in a baseball cap continued
clicking the mouse. Embarrassed, I rushed away.

How can I help this poor boy? I wondered as I paced
the floor. *He's poisoning his mind.*

Then a battle began stirring. I heard a quiet whisper that
conflicted with my strong desire to help. "This isn't any of
your business." Feeling like a nosy intruder, I returned to
the boy's side.

"What are you looking at?" and "How old are you?" I
blurted out in one long, panicky breath.

"Fourteen," he answered smugly, staring at the screen.

As I continued pacing, I decided to appeal to his logic. "Because you're under 21, it's against the law for you to be looking at this stuff on the computer. This is not good for you."

I sighed heavily, bent forward slightly, and peered into his eyes hidden beneath his cap. No response, just silence and glimpses of pain.

Just then, the librarian stepped into our path. I explained my concern while she listened carefully. "What is your understanding about the law?" I asked.

"I don't know, but I'll find out," she stammered, then whisked off to investigate.

The young victim quickly signed off and nervously gathered his books into his backpack, preparing to escape. Would I let him walk away pretending nothing had happened? In a split second I resolved not to give up and trotted after him.

"You know, this is so destructive it could hurt you for the rest of your life. And I bet your parents wouldn't like you doing this either." As a mother of two teenage boys, my heart ached for him.

"Well, you don't even know me," he snapped.

"You're right." I took another deep breath trying to calm myself. "I don't know you, but God does." I persisted. "God knows everything about you. He loves you very much, and He isn't pleased with this because you're hurting yourself."

The library supervisor appeared just in time to justify the boy's offense. She stated, "There's really nothing we can do about this. It's not against the law and many people come here to do this." Then thrusting her hand on her hip, she stretched her neck forward and scolded me, "That's why they have privacy screens on the computer!"

The young man marched off quickly. Embarrassed, I slunk off to the geography section to join my twelve-year-old daughter. I tried helping her gather information for her research project, but my mind kept racing. Why don't they put a stop to this? I should write a protest letter. I felt heartsick.

When I glanced up, the freckled face prisoner of pornography was standing before me. I jerked back, startled. "Thank you for stopping me," he mumbled, hanging his head low. "I really don't like doing that; sometimes I just can't help myself."

Compassion flooded me. "Oh, I believe you," I assured him.

Without taking time to form my thoughts, my words came gently tumbling out. "Do you know Jesus? He's the only One who can really help you overcome this." I didn't worry about saying the right words.

I pulled out two chairs at a nearby table and invited him to sit down. First, he introduced himself as Matt and then explained how he attends church regularly, a private school, and also a Christian youth organization. He didn't talk about having a personal relationship with Jesus Christ.

"You need to be totally honest about this problem," I advised him. "Perhaps your mom or someone who cares about you in your youth group can help you. Ask for their help and their prayers."

"Okay, I will," he nodded. Then he added shamefully, "I think I'm addicted or something."

"Well, Matt, it's very common for this to start at your age, and it can only get worse. The devil wants to keep you right where he has you," I warned, "But you can overcome him and have victory over this."

We stepped outside the library to a quiet spot that chilly, gray afternoon. "Matt, God has big plans for you. He's watching over your life very carefully. He wants to set you free from this terrible bondage. May I pray for you?"

After praying with Matt, asking God to draw him close to Jesus and give him victory over his addiction, I noted a glimpse of hope in his eyes. I softly patted his shoulder. "I'm sure you'll be a powerful man of God someday."

Just then, his mother drove up. "Thanks for everything," he smiled, and hurried off. His step seemed lighter.

I drove home, feeling a little relief for Matt, but angry toward our legal system. The pornographic giant parading on the Internet had struck another innocent child. Slamming my fist on the steering wheel, I cried out, "What should I do?"

In the silence of my car, I heard a gentle answer. "If you will keep sharing the truth, I will set my people free." Tears filled my eyes. I remembered just a few years earlier when my situation appeared hopeless and a godly woman cared enough to share the Gospel with me. Her loving counsel combined with God's Word saved my marriage and family.

As my peace returned, I made an even deeper, heartfelt commitment to share God's Word whenever and wherever I see an opportunity. I'm relieved to say it didn't lead me to anymore pornography victims, but it did lead me to teach a girls' Bible study for my daughter and her friends. They are learning truths that set them free from the world's deceptions and protect their minds from Satan's traps.

Two years later, my prayer remains the same, "Lord, who ever you put in my path, help me to show them your compassion, and give me the courage to speak the truth in love."

Discussion Questions

1. How does God's Word describe the lost?

2. 2 Timothy 2:26

2 Corinthians 4:4

Ephesians 2:1-3

1 Corinthians 2:14

2. "The worst sin towards our fellow creatures is not to hate them, but to be indifferent to them; that is the essence of inhumanity" (G. Bernard Shaw). How did Debbie show love for Matt while hating the sin of pornography?

3. Do you agree or disagree with Debbie's attempt to help this young man? Why or why not?

4. Do you think all believers should step out of their comfort zone to get involved with unbelievers struggling with addictions? Why or why not?

If you encounter someone who struggles with pornography, consider offering help through the following websites: www.bebroken.com and www.xxxchurch.com.

*When Christ said: "I was hungry and you fed me," he
didn't mean only the hunger for bread and food; he
also meant the hunger to be loved. —Mother Teresa*

Honk 'n Holler

John Murphy as told to Pamela Enderby

*"Is not this the kind of fasting I have chosen ... to share
your food with the hungry" (Isaiah 58:6).*

On the evening news, a Salvation Army spokesman was
pleading for volunteers to help feed the hungry and homeless. It aroused my compassion. I considered the people
born and reared in difficult situations. Due to no fault of
their own, they live in poverty without skills and opportunities to succeed.

I decided to pitch in and help. On Tuesday evenings, I
jump on board the Salvation Army's cargo van with a hand-
ful of other volunteers. Upon reaching various city parks
and public libraries in downtown Kansas City, Missouri, we
park, honk the horn, and holler, "Hot food! Hot food!" The
homeless run toward us like ravished wolves. They push
each other to get first in line for hot food, a sandwich, coffee, or Gatorade. Their food, coupled with our brief words,
"God bless you," and "God loves you," offer some comfort,

but lack of time keeps us from engaging in personal conversations, much needed deliverance, and healing prayers.

After several months of feeding the homeless, I was compelled to do more than offer food and a meager blessing. One particular evening, an unsightly beggar arrested my attention. He was alone and trembling in his green stocking cap and tattered flannel shirt. The compassion of Christ drove me to do something I had never done before.

First, I asked another volunteer to take my place doling out food. Then, pushing my way through the crowd, I got close enough to meet Ed, a modern day leper. Ed's sores were filled with pus and blood. His body odor, wafting through his ragged clothes, sent chills through my body. For nearly 20 years, Ed had made his home under a bridge. Society labeled him "untouchable."

I asked Ed if I could pray for him. Ed agreed, so I gently placed my hands near his sores and started in. I pleaded for what I believed God had in His heart for this man. "Lord, please have mercy on Ed. Fill him with faith and hope to turn to You for help. Please set him free of alcoholism."

Week after week, I returned to Ed's side and slowly gained his trust. I listened to him recount painful stories from his past and continued to pray for him. Though I didn't see radical physical improvements, he eventually took his first step of faith and prayed to receive Christ.

I believed in a better future for Ed, but my peers tried convincing me otherwise. They shared somber stories of homeless men and women who heard the Scriptures, accepted Christ as their Savior, and even received prayer ministry, but to no avail. Rarely did any one gain enough confidence and strength to seek out organizations offering jobs, homes, and temporary financial support. They choose poverty instead of freedom. Some even committed suicide. I agonized over the possibility of watching Ed choose a similar destructive path.

After several more weeks of praying with Ed and building a friendship with him, he disappeared. No one could tell me of his whereabouts. For days, I grieved. I couldn't put Ed out of my mind. I continued to carry him in my heart.

After Ed's disappearance, I continued to reach out to more homeless, spiritually hungry souls like Ed. I could rarely see any change in their lives no matter how many meals they received. Quite often, I grew discouraged. Their needs frequently drove me to the throne of grace. I prayed for power equal to the task.

About a year later, the authorities at the alcohol treatment center informed me that Ed admitted himself for treatment and succeeded in remaining dry. He also ran into good fortune; his relatives died and left a generous inheritance. Unlike most homeless people experiencing a financial break, Ed invested in a home and settled down to start a new life.

Learning about Ed's victory infused me with fresh hope that God not only knows and cares about the homeless, but also is capable of rescuing and delivering them. No matter how downtrodden and despairing a situation, God's grace is greater. Someday, this side of heaven, I hope to see Ed again.

I'm inspired to keep helping the homeless when I recall Jesus' words in Matthew 25:35. "For I was hungry and you gave me something to eat, I was thirsty and you gave me something to drink, I was a stranger and you invited me in." When I stop to linger in His presence, I can almost hear Him whisper, "Thank you for doing this to me."

"Heavenly Father, keep heaping your compassion for the homeless upon my heart. Help me see their fears and offer them hope to dream and aspire to succeed. May I always see You in every person."

Discussion Questions

1. Jesus gave respect to people his culture called "losers." How did John show respect to Ed?

2. John sometimes felt overwhelmed by the needs of one "untouchable." What kept John from quitting?

3. John learned that most homeless people remain unchanged after they receive food and prayer on a regular basis. Why should we continue to reach out to them?

4. Psalm 82:3-4 commands, "Defend the cause of the weak and fatherless; maintain the rights of the poor and oppressed. Rescue the weak and needy; deliver them from the hand of the wicked." If you step out of your comfort zone to become a rescuer and defender of people, what may it require of you?

Love is the power that moves you to give to another
person with no expectation of reward.
—Lewis Smedes

Love Never Fails

Pamela Enderby

"Love your enemies, do good to them, and lend to them
without expecting to get anything back" (Luke 6:35).

A week before Thanksgiving, my husband John and his college buddy Tim scouted out the run down central district of St. Paul, Minnesota. It was Tim's idea. Growing up as a missionary in Hong Kong had cultivated his desire to feed the poor and hungry. Although John and I considered ourselves "poor" college students without much to give, we agreed to help with this outreach.

A dilapidated diner grabbed Tim's attention. "Let's go in."

Tim gently pushed open the wrinkled screen door dangling from its rusty hinges. A mass of flies flitted from table to table, sipping leftover food.

"What can I do for you?" asked an elderly lady, bent over, mopping the floor.

"We'll have a cup of coffee." Tim answered, politely. The coffee poured out jet-black, thick like gravy.

"We're serving a free turkey dinner at my apartment on Thanksgiving Day," said Tim. "We can feed five homeless people. Would you get the word out?"

"I'll see what I can do," she said, in a gravelly voice.

On Thanksgiving, I peered through Tim's apartment window. Four shabbily dressed guests shuffled up the sidewalk. My stomach did somersaults.

"Please, Lord, help me show these people Your love." My anxiety soared the moment they stepped into the apartment. Trying to hide my uneasiness, I grabbed a pot of hot coffee and began to serve them. Within minutes their hearts opened.

The old woman, Marion, shared painful memories of growing up in an orphanage. Her voice crackled with sorrow. Suddenly her mood switched as she reminisced of past boyfriends. Her flirtatious, falling-in-love stories teased the bedraggled men sitting across the room. They reciprocated by flashing her toothless smiles and calling her "Sweetheart" and "Sugar Plum."

Paul, appearing as though he hadn't eaten for days, shared his sordid story about his dying mother in Duluth. He longed to be at her side, but skimpy finances deterred him.

George, a husky man, slumping in the corner of the couch, recounted the mornings selling newspapers in sub-zero temperatures. Pangs of guilt struck me. Many days I complained about walking one block to catch the city bus for work.

Bill, heavy set and balding, remained quiet and paced the room like a trapped animal. I attempted to settle his restlessness by assigning him the table-setting job, but he resisted. At one point he left the apartment to walk around the block, and he returned reeking of tobacco.

Finally, it was time to settle around our makeshift dining room table—three card tables pushed together. Tim requested we bow our heads and give thanks for the food and for each guest. They shoveled food into their mouths with childlike groans that hummed with satisfaction. I had worried needlessly about preparing too much food. A 25-pound turkey, dressing, corn, 10 pounds of potatoes, Jell-O salad, and rolls.

After dinner, with filled stomachs, warmed hearts, and food clinging to the men's unshaven beards, Tim took a bold step and passed out hymnbooks. Between off-key songs this homely, ragamuffin choir shared more hardships. I felt compassion swelling in my heart.

Finally, Bill, the young, discontent fellow, had had enough chatter and singing. He insisted on going "home" to his 9'x12' motel room, and cajoled the others to follow suit. I felt more compassion swelling as I watched them pull on their oversized, worn coats. We exchanged warm handshakes before they shuffled out the door.

In the car Paul shared more sad stories of his sick mother living in Duluth. Moved with compassion, Tim drove Paul to the Greyhound bus station to purchase a ticket for him to visit her. When he left the train station, turning to wave one final good-bye, Tim spotted Paul exchanging his $15.00 ticket for a $5 bill.

Upon hearing this report, my budding compassion withered. "We sacrificed an entire day serving those beggars. And we spent our hard-earned college funds buying them food," I whined. "How could Paul be so devious?"

For days I entertained critical thoughts. *Sure, God tells us to feed the poor and hungry, but shouldn't we at least have received one word of thanks?* I entertained reasons for Paul's deceptive behavior—an addictive craving for tobacco or alcohol. But my assumptions failed to appease me.

Meanwhile, Jesus' words in John 25:35 played over and over in my mind. "For I was hungry and you gave me something to eat, I was thirsty and you gave me something to drink, I was a stranger and you invited me in."

These Scriptures began to soften my heart. Finally, I confessed my selfishness and once again, Jesus revealed His unrelenting love to me. While I was a sinner, Christ died on a cross for me whether I ever love Him in return. When I don't live up to His standards, He doesn't judge me because He didn't come to judge but to save me from my sins and failures. The truth of His salvation shined brilliantly.

Suddenly I could see Paul through Jesus' eyes. Paul, too, is a sinner Jesus died for. He stands in need of forgiveness just as I do. Instead of judging him, I began to pray for him.

Genuine love comes with a price tag. God calls us to love others in practical and even uncomfortable ways, regardless of whether we receive socially appropriate rewards. The question I am learning to ask myself is, "What am I willing to pay?" For Jesus the cost was loving me enough to die.

How can we ever love too much?

Discussion Questions

1. Have you ever been "duped" in an outreach attempt? Explain your situation.

2. Harboring disappointment leads to self-pity and resentment that can squelch us from stepping out of our comfort zone for future outreach attempts. How is it possible to overcome these obstacles?

3. Dr. Bob Smith states, "Ninety percent of evangelism is love." The Bible uses two words for love, "phileo" and "agape." Phileo is a love that is reciprocated, a mutual love that flows two ways. Agape love is a love of sacrifices. Agape expresses an outgoing, selfless giving that loves, expecting nothing in return. The miracle of agape love begins to blossom in our hearts after we

choose to forgive. How do the following verses teach us to love with agape love?

Matthew 5:38-48

Romans 5:6-8

I John 3:16-18

I John 4:16, 5:1-2

4. Mother Teresa states, "Love until it hurts; it takes deep sacrifices to proclaim the Word of God." What sacrifices are you willing to make to demonstrate God's love?

~

Obstacle Four: I'm Spiritually Unfit.

"For my thoughts are not your thoughts, neither are
your ways my ways," declares the Lord. "As the heav-
ens are higher than the earth, so are my ways higher
than your ways, and my thoughts than your
thoughts."

(Isaiah 55:8-9)

God uses people with hearts turned toward Him.
Past sins and failures are forgiven. When we open
our hearts in obedient faith to His will, He uses us.
Jesus has a job for you to do, and no one else can take
your place. —Charles Stanley

Stronger When Broken

Judy Majewski as told to Pamela Enderby

"God … comforts us in all our troubles, so that we can
comfort those in any trouble" (2 Corinthians 1:3-4).

God frequently interrupts my life with gentle nudgings to comfort, counsel, and encourage the brokenhearted. They need someone to identify with their pain and failures because they feel ashamed and alone.

I know, because as a young adult, I was like them. For years, I hid like a slimy larva in a cocoon, deluging myself with alcohol, drugs, and promiscuity. Then, growing into my late thirties, I surrendered full ownership of my life to God and experienced His marvelous forgiveness and unconditional love.

Now, years later, God is using me, working as a chiropractor's assistant to offer help and hope to others whose lives are headed for destruction. One afternoon, at the office, Lisa came shuffling in, crying. She required frequent therapy from a car accident. Guiding her to the back room for an ultrasound, she looked unusually sad.

"What's bothering you?" I asked, gently.

"I'm having trouble with my boyfriend," she began to sob.

"May I pray with you? I think that might help."

Lisa resisted.

"Well, think it over," I smiled. "I'd be happy to pray with you anytime."

Over several months of visits, I tried cheering Lisa with uplifting conversations, but words failed to cut through her depression.

Finally, the time came during one of Lisa's therapy sessions when I felt led to tell her about my past depression. When my son was killed in a car accident, I hit rock bottom, and then for years I tried to escape life by using alcohol and drugs. Finally, I cried out to God for His help, and He pulled me out of the miry pit.

"How can you be so happy when you lost your son in a car accident?" Lisa cried.

"I don't see Scott as dead, but alive in Heaven." I said. "Scott came to know Christ as His Savior shortly before He died. That's why I have peace."

"I'll never get over my loss," she said, her body trembling. "I just had an abortion." Again, I explained how God's healing power in my life freed me from shame after having an abortion at age 15. "After you confess your sin to God and try to go back to talk to Him about it, He says, 'I don't remember that.' He removes our sins as far as the East is from the West. He doesn't remember them anymore!" I looked her in the eye, placed my hand over hers and asked, "Would you like to receive God's forgiveness right now?"

As Lisa bowed her head, more tears flowed while she quietly confessed her sins to God. "I never felt anybody cared about me until now," she said, wiping her cheeks. "Thank you for helping me find God's forgiveness."

The following week Lisa showed up for another treatment. "I've never been so happy in my whole life!" she exclaimed. She had already left her boyfriend and began pursuing a completely different lifestyle. Her face beamed with God's light. Today, Lisa walks in complete healing from post-abortion trauma, she attends church regularly, and she enjoys a growing relationship with God.

Discussion Questions

1. Isaiah 43:25 states, "I, even I, am he who blots out your transgressions, for my own sake, and remembers your sins no more." Paraphrase this verse. How does it relate to your past?

2. Have you received God's forgiveness for your past failures? Have you forgiven yourself?

3. God never wastes our broken pieces. Do you view your past mistakes as opportunities to share God's healing message of forgiveness and unconditional love? Why or why not?

4. According to 2 Corinthians 1:3-4, Paul admonishes us to comfort others with the comfort we have received from God. What comfort have you received from God during a time of distress that you might share with an unbeliever?

5. After offering your past mistakes to God, begin asking Him to use you as His messenger of forgiveness, grace, and mercy to the helpless and hurting.

The power that produces fruitfulness comes from our
love relationship with Jesus and from no other source.
—John Piper

Help! I'm Spiritually Dry

Debbie Williams as told to Pamela Enderby

"If a man remains in me and I in him, he will bear much
fruit; apart from me you can do nothing" (John 15:5).

For months I sensed God calling, "Debbie, come back."
My job and my friends had consumed my time. Sure, I
glanced at Scripture occasionally and prayed perfunctory
prayers on the way to work, but slowly my relationship
with God had withered. If I were to rate it on a scale from
one to ten, I'd give myself a one.

Trying times with family and friends drove me back to
God. I knew He was the only One who could help me un-
tangle my problems. I aimed at setting aside time every day
for prayer, Bible study, and journaling. Changing my lifestyle and developing new habits didn't come easy or
quickly, but it was well worth it.

Over time, I felt peace and joy, and my quiet times
turned from drudgery to the most delightful time in my day.
And that's not all. God began to use me to be salt and light.

One afternoon, several months after reconnecting with God, I packed my Bible study, *Experiencing God*, and the three kids I was baby-sitting, and headed for Discovery Zone, an indoor playground. I kept one eye on the children and the other on my study. A nice looking man in his thirties seated about two tables away caught my attention. Glancing up, I steadied myself for his approach.

After introducing himself, he inquired. "What are you reading?" Rather than give him a straight answer, I pitched him a simple explanation of my spiritual journey. Jim appeared calm and interested. Then while proceeding to explain how this book was helping me cultivate intimacy with God, his eyebrows suddenly shot up and his face grew tense. He erupted and began venting angry words toward God, his ex-wife, and even himself. As I listened to this angry unbeliever tell stories about life's injustices, I tried sympathizing with his pain, but mostly, I felt terribly helpless. Not knowing what to say, the first and only thing that came to mind was, "Would you like to attend church with me on Sunday? I think you'll find some hope and comfort there."

The following Sunday, Jim surprised me and showed up. Eventually he got involved in our singles' ministry and developed a few close friendships. They ministered God's unconditional love to him and eventually, over a period of months, he experienced Jesus' forgiveness. As I watched Jim's spiritual journey unfold, it fueled my desire to continue sharing my faith.

It happened at the most unpredictable times and with the most unusual people. For example, every Monday after work, I carve out a "date night with God," and enjoy a hot meal at a restaurant while doing my Bible study. One evening a customer approached me while I was eating dinner. "May I sit down?" he asked.

"Sure, pull up a chair."

"What are you reading?"

By now I was into a different study. I slid my *Search for Significance* within his reach and began to share. "I used to let the world's standards dictate how I felt about myself. Now, I'm beginning to understand that the more I receive God's love and acceptance, the more self-worth I gain."

He stiffened and immediately rose from his chair. I kept silent, expecting him to leave. Instead, he started crying. "I've attempted suicide 27 times and here I am. You say my life has purpose?" He threw up his hands and slumped back down in his chair. "Tell me more," he said.

Fumbling for words, I grabbed my Bible. This man desperately needed to hear about God's unfailing love. I read to him portions of Psalm 139.

The Scriptures seemed to calm him. He listened intently and occasionally heaved heavy sighs. I felt an intense desire to see him saved. If only he would say "yes" to Jesus, right here, I thought. However, the opposite happened.

I shared John 3:16: "For God so loved the world that he gave his one and only Son, that whoever believes in him shall not perish but have eternal life." Then he abruptly broke in. "I'm a Muslim, and I'll always be a Muslim."

The fiery look in his eyes frightened me. I recoiled as I listened to him defend his religion.

God's love for this Muslim man gives me hope for his future. I'm praying that someday he'll understand and accept the Truth.

I'm learning that the more I sit in Jesus' presence, feeding my soul with His Word, He imprints His very image upon me. His peace, joy, and love radiating from me draws others to me. There's nothing more exciting.

Discussion Questions

1. Someone stated, "Unless we have invested a great deal of time in our secret ministry to the Lord, the shallowness of our public ministry will be very evi-

dent." How would you rate your walk with God on a scale from 1 to 10?

2. In John 15:4 Jesus tells us to "remain" in Him. Explain what that means to you.

3. We can have intimacy with God by caring about what He cares about. What lifestyle change(s) could improve your intimacy with God?

4. According to Galatians 5:22-23, we read about the fruit of the Holy Spirit that flows from us when we remain in Jesus. List the fruit, then give specific examples of how this fruit, expressed through you, might draw the lost to Jesus. Consider Ephesians 4:32, Luke 6:27-31, and Titus 3:1-2 for application ideas.

5. Spending time in God's Word prepares us to share our faith. What spiritual truth(s) have you recently received that you could share with an unbeliever? (Use words an unbeliever can understand.) Pray for an opportunity to share that truth this week with an unbeliever.

God is my Defender, while my heart is my accuser.
—Martin Luther

An Opportunity Missed

John Murphy as told to Pamela Enderby

"If our heart condemns us, God is greater than our heart,
and knows all things" (I John 3:20 NKJV).

My wife Pat and I had enjoyed a week's vacation relax-
ing in the majestic Colorado Mountains. After one last good
night's rest, we packed our bags and left our motel room,
lighthearted, happy, and hungry. Walking across the street,
ready to eat breakfast at the local restaurant, the waitress
met us at the door. "You'll have to wait 45 minutes to be
served," she stated. Little did we know, this delay was putting us on a path to teach me an unforgettable outreach lesson.

After driving awhile we spotted a small diner in Oakley,
Kansas and pulled in. From outward appearances, the place
looked suitable. As we stepped inside the restaurant, a smiling waitress led us to a booth in the non-smoking section.
We relaxed, sipped coffee, and chuckled over the town's
trademark: "Home of the largest prairie dogs in the world."

Suddenly, everything changed. Tension filled the air when two of the roughest looking guys we had ever seen pushed their way through the restaurant door. Their tattooed arms bulged out of their black tee shirts. One guy with a bushy beard and wearing a bandana, black pants, and leather boots probably weighed 250 pounds and reached 6'3". I imagined him sweeping the place clean without sparing anyone's life!

Slouching into the booth next to ours, they pulled cigarettes from their pockets. Cigarette smoke quickly filled the place and annoyed us, but we didn't dare complain. The last thing we wanted to do was offend them. So we picked up our mugs and moved like mice, as inconspicuously as possible, to a booth across the room. We felt at ease there, at least for a while.

About half way through breakfast, a troubling thought interrupted me. "Offer to buy their meal and ask them if they know Jesus." Immediately, every fiber of my flesh rebelled against the idea. You've gotta be kidding. In my eyes those guys resembled giant Goliaths capable of tearing me apart. I had hoped the nagging thought would disappear, but it didn't. It only grew stronger, and I grew more tense.

We gulped our breakfast, paid our bill, and quickly slipped out of the restaurant. While driving down the road, we prayed for the two men, but the guilt of failing to witness tugged on my heart. Playing the scene over and over in my mind, I realized how God had carefully redirected our steps so that we might share His love.

A missed opportunity? Yes. Is God angry with me? In my opinion, He should be. After all, He directed our steps that we might offer these needy souls a touch of His love. Jesus said, "My sheep listen to my voice; I know them, and they follow me" (John 10:27). Instead, I blew Him off and played it safe.

My heart accused me. They might end up in hell and it's all your fault!

That's when God's spirit quickened my heart with the truth, defending me. "Yes, John, you could have ministered to those guys. Next time, you'll do it, won't you?" Amazing! I thought. God is more like a loving coach, encouraging me, rather than an angry boss. God's mercy and grace offered me comfort, not condemnation. Silently, I asked God to forgive me for chickening out. My heaviness lifted.

I'll never forget this outreach lesson. It takes a humble heart to listen and obey what God tells me to say and do, but even when I mess up, He never points an accusing finger at me. Instead, He comes to pick me up, brush me off, and encourage me once again to be His witness. I'm so thankful God does more than forgive my mistakes. He erases them!

Discussion Questions

1. Have you ever intentionally missed an opportunity to share your faith? How did you feel about yourself? What does 1 Corinthians 2:4 say? How does it apply?

2. Have you taken your missed opportunities to God? Will you receive His forgiveness? What does Psalm 32:5 and 1 John 1:9 promise?

3. Missionary Jim Elliot, stated, "Delayed obedience creates a seedbed for doubt and fear." How can this truth apply to outreach?

4. Think of someone you're hesitant to reach out to now because you blew off a witnessing opportunity. If you risk sharing your faith, what might be the worst possible response you encounter?

5. When it comes to witnessing, why is "the greatest risk not taking one?"

*The shocking message of the Bible continues to be
that God has chosen the least of all vessels to do his
greatest work. —Tim Hansel*

Victory in my Disability

Virgean Bosworth as told to Pamela Enderby

*"My message and my preaching were ... with a
demonstration of the Spirit's power" (1 Corinthians 2:4).*

The thrill of watching my fiancé compete at motor
cross races enticed me to give it a whirl. So one afternoon, I
revved up my motorcycle's 125-cc engine and sped for the
dirt track. Approaching a steep hill, I increased speed,
skimmed its crest, then suddenly lost control. I landed hard
and bounced on the rocky, dry ground for several yards.
Without the protection of a helmet, I was left with a broken
body and shattered dreams to match. My professional dancing career was over and so was my engagement. No one
wanted a 22-year-old who resembled a walking, talking
toddler.

The following four years I endured physical rehabilita-
tion and speech therapy. When I finally regained enough
strength and self-confidence, I returned to college. Although professional dancing was out of the question, I still

felt passionate about it so I majored in dramatics. After graduating, I began my job search.

Frequently I cried out to God. "I can't do much, but I will be faithful with the things I'm able to do. Please help me find a job."

The following summer, I filled a part-time position at a Montessori school. It was a test of endurance. Every weekday for three months, at 6:30 a.m., I wobbled to work on my three-wheel bicycle.

Working with small children satisfied my longing to feel useful. But one early morning, upon arriving to work, the school director released me. "Virgean, I'm sorry, but you don't have enough coordination to be a teacher's assistant." He was right. My tilted, wobbly body could hardly sit comfortably on the ground with the kids or on their small chairs.

The next day, I climbed onto my bike to job hunt again. Inhaling the cool, crisp autumn air filled me with a renewed sense of hope and courage. I desperately wanted and needed to earn more money than my meager disability check offered.

Peddling slowly down Main Street, I reached a grocery store with a help wanted sign in the window. The manager glanced at my resume after sizing me up. "There's nothing you can do here." His words felt like knives piercing my flesh.

Growing up, my parents modeled perseverance during tough times and drilled their "no quitter" attitude into me. So I continued on, limping down the street, into the shoe store, then the drug store. Every proprietor I approached that day spoke the same cutting words, "We can't use you." I cried all the way home, feeling like an over-educated bum.

In my second week of job searching, I passed a nursing home. Childhood memories of visiting my grandmother filled my mind. I can't. I can't go in there, I thought. I had seen enough crippled old people. My stomach churned.

They wouldn't want me anyway. I'm not much better off than they are. For some reason I entered the nursing home. The director of nursing hired me on the spot.

Working as the activities director three days a week, I quickly got bored asking the patients "reality questions" such as, "What did you eat for lunch?" and "What day is it today?" Writing their comments legibly demanded more skill than I had and most of the time my job felt meaningless.

I had nowhere else to go so, again, I cried out to God. "Now, what do I do?" The One who had rescued me before came to my aid once again. He didn't give me a new job, but He changed my heart.

First, He began by opening my eyes to the residents' hollow stares and empty hearts. I grew more and more aware that they needed to hear about God's love, compassion, and kindness. Second, I had difficulty putting my faith in words, but I had a small amount of musical talent to help express myself. God reminded me to use it for His glory. So I volunteered two days a week to sing hymns and plunk out tunes on the piano for anyone who would come to listen! Although I couldn't hit the notes right all the time, the music seemed to comfort the residents and for the first time in a long time, I experienced heartfelt joy.

One evening before leaving work, the nursing home director stopped me. "Some residents are complaining about your religious views," she said. "When the patients are agitated, the nurses have to work harder. This will have to stop."

"I'm sure some of the patients enjoy my company," I responded, a bit defensively. "May I continue to visit them?"

She fixed me with a glare. "From now on, you'll have to get permission from the residents' supervisor before you visit with anyone."

Immediately, rejection and disappointment revisited my heart. Again, I cried to God for help. During my past sufferings, I learned I must lean harder on God for His power to pull me through. When I did, He strengthened me to remain faithful to His plan for my life.

I boldly approached my supervisor, apologizing for upsetting anyone and asked for her permission to visit three specific residents who I thought had enjoyed my company. She granted my wishes.

As my visits and friendships grew with those three, I felt a growing desire to visit others. While asking God who they might be, I also asked Him for favor with the nursing home supervisor.

As I waited for God's direction, John M.'s name kept coming to mind, but I resisted. I can't visit him. John, heavy set and unshaven, was the last person I wanted to get near. In my opinion, he was just a dirty old man and the orderlies made it clear they thought so too. They often teased him, "Hey, John, have you found any good looking women yet?"

"No, not yet, but I'm still looking," he'd chuckle. John's slurred, gruff voice made him difficult to understand.

Eventually, I gave in to God and pushed through my uneasiness. With the residents' supervisor's permission, I began sharing Scriptures with John. At first, the Scriptures seemed to fly right over his head. He stared blankly at the wall whenever I read from the Bible. I often felt I was wasting my time, but his invitations to come back kept me returning.

After seven months, I decided to end my visits with John because I had grown discouraged. I figured I had spent enough time offering him God's Word while seeing little signs of interest. The day I went into his room to say I wouldn't be coming back, John surprised me and asked me to sing a song. He didn't ask for any particular song, so I started with a familiar hymn, the words flowing freely and sweetly.

God's love filled John's room and his heart that afternoon, and from that point on, his interest in God's Word seemed to grow. Finally, his heart was softening.

Weeks later, while John and I were visiting, an orderly passed his room and bellowed his usual disgusting question, "John, have you found any women yet?" I grimaced for fear of John's usual response.

Then, to my surprise, he responded resolutely and clearly, "No, I've given that up. I'm chasing the Lord now!"

In my eagerness to see John saved, I leapt out of my chair and hugged him. "John, do you want to become a Christian?" I had often read and explained that God desired him to come into His kingdom. I quoted Colossians 1:12-13 to him, "Joyfully giving thanks to the Father, who has qualified you to share in the inheritance of the saints in the kingdom of light ... he has rescued us from the dominion of darkness and brought us into the kingdom of the Son he loves, in whom we have redemption, the forgiveness of sins."

Hunched over in his wheelchair, in that stale nursing home, John lifted his voice to the Lord, asking for forgiveness. This time, his slurred, gruff words sounded like music to my ears. My spirit soared.

"You're my brother now, and I'm your sister!" I clapped my hands, rejoicing.

"Glory to God," he praised, thrusting his arms in the air. God had breathed life into John's spirit.

Thirty years have passed now since my accident. Some days I feel absolutely useless and trapped in a dark tunnel. My words and actions are still defective. But then God amazes me. When I call upon His resurrection power, my absolute insufficiency invokes God's total sufficiency. Time and again, He walks me through my valley of despair. My disability provides for the triumph of His divine power, and I'm learning that I can still be a blessing for those called to inherit eternal life.

Discussion Questions

1. How did Virgean overcome her physical and emotional limitations?

2. What personal benefits did Virgean receive by sharing her faith in the nursing home?

3. You don't have to be disabled to feel disabled when it comes to sharing your faith. In Ephesians 1:19, the apostle Paul states that we have God's resurrection power living within us. How did it make a difference in Virgean's witness? How can it make a difference in yours?

4. It was the work of the Holy Spirit coupled with Scripture that persuaded John M. that he needed Jesus, not Virgean's persuasive words. Why is using Scripture sometimes our best method of witnessing? Read Hebrews 4:12.

5. Read Psalm 138:3. If your evangelistic endeavors look hopeless, how is God encouraging you today?

The wire is you and I; the current is God. We have the power to let the current pass through us, use us, and produce the light of the world–Jesus. —Mother Teresa

The Gospel According to Mr. Goodwrench

Esther Brandt as told to Pamela Enderby

"The Spirit gives life; the flesh counts for nothing" (John 6:63).

Every Saturday morning, Jim stormed through my front door with a plethora of Bible questions. He rapidly fired them like a television game show host. "If the Bible is true, where did Adam's kids find people to marry? Do you really believe Jonah was in the belly of a whale?" He figured I had all the answers because I had mentored his girlfriend, Sandee. To be honest, at times, I groped for answers.

"Since Adam and Eve were the first (and only) human beings, their children would have had no other choice than to intermarry," I explained. "God did not forbid inter-family marriage until much later when there were enough people for it to be unnecessary."

113

In my opinion, a lot of Jim's questions seemed irrelevant to finding Jesus. Fortunately, my limited Bible knowledge satisfied him most of the time; however when I was stumped, I'd investigate the internet and other resources. Later I realized that by asking strange questions, Jim was carving out his personal pathway to Jesus.

One morning, Sandee called me at work, "Jim wants to meet with us tonight. He has more questions." Excitement filled her voice. "I have a feeling he's going to get saved today," she added. "Let's have dinner together after work."

I hung up the phone and began rummaging through my purse, hoping to find the Four Spiritual Laws pamphlet I thought was safely tucked in the zippered compartment of my purse. The only paper I found was a crumpled gum wrapper. Rushing to get to work on time, I had also forgotten my Bible. I panicked.

Willie Mae can surely help me out of this tight spot, I thought. Willie Mae was one of the clerks in my accounting department who never hid her love for the Lord. Christian posters decorated her office walls and quiet hymns drifted from her cubicle every time I passed by.

But that morning, Willie Mae had also failed to bring to work her spiritual arsenal. "Don't you worry, Esther," she assured me. "I'll call my church for help." As her church secretary dictated the Salvation Scriptures, word for word, Willie Mae wrote them down. I tucked them in my pocket and briskly returned to work.

All day long, computer entry problems demanded my attention. Just when I'd attempt to pull out the Scriptures to brush up on the Gospel presentation, one employee after another would call for help. I left work with a pounding headache and a knot in the pit of my stomach.

"Lord, I didn't even have my quiet time this morning," I moaned, weaving through rush hour traffic. "How can I possibly share the Gospel? I'm worn out and I'm not prepared! I just want to go home." Whining never changed

God's mind in the past, but I tried it again, hoping God would somehow keep Sandee and Jim from showing up.

When I arrived at the restaurant, I collapsed in a corner booth and escaped in my dream world. I daydreamed of going home, kicking off my shoes, and unwinding. Maybe I'd try a new recipe or clean a closet. Putting my hands to creating or organizing usually helped calm me after a hectic day.

Within a few minutes, Jim shuffled in carrying a pile of pamphlets. He sat down across from me, grinning ear to ear. Before he could utter a word, Sandee flopped down next to me, unloading, non-stop, the events of her busy day. Sandee's chatter coupled with Jim's fidgeting and table tapping exacerbated my frazzled nerves.

Finally Sandee paused, and Jim piped up. "See these pamphlets?" He handled them carefully like a valuable treasure. "When my car broke down this morning, I took it to the GM Goodwrench garage and found them in the waiting room. They talk about God's love and how to receive forgiveness."

"I have a few questions," he said, still smiling. "I underlined the Bible verses I like best, but I don't understand exactly what they mean," he said, pointing to the same salvation verses Willie Mae handed me that morning.

At that point, the obvious hit me. God had everything under control. It didn't matter how weak and spiritually unfit I was feeling. God makes no mistakes. I had spent the entire day fretting for nothing!

Clearing my throat, I stumbled through explanations, digging deep into my heart for the right words, now trusting God to help Jim understand. Jim listened intently and remained quiet. When I finished, he collected his pamphlets and I breathed a sigh of relief, knowing I had fulfilled my obligation. Finally, I could go home and clean my linen closet!

Jim's voice interrupted my plan when I heard him say, "I want to ask Jesus into my life." Jim, Sandee, and I stepped outside the restaurant and squeezed together on a stone bench. The three of us held hands and bowed our heads. I had the privilege of leading Jim through the sinner's prayer.* I was thrilled listening to this man surrender his life to Christ and equally humbled that God had allowed me to play a small part in His sovereign plan.

I drove home in amazement. My outreach perspective shifted dramatically. God proved to me He is greater than my spiritual inadequacies. He has a plan and He can make it happen. He goes to all extremes to make it happen! He brings sinners into His kingdom by guiding and using even ordinary, spiritually unprepared people like me. The most recent question I'm challenged to ask myself is, "Am I willing to let God use me no matter how spiritually unprepared I feel?"

* If you're given the opportunity to pray the "sinner's prayer" with an unbeliever, it may sound something like this: "Dear Lord Jesus, I realize that I am a sinner and I am truly sorry for my sins. I accept the fact that You died for me on the Cross. I ask You to come live in my heart as my Savior and Lord of my life. Please take full control of me and help me to become the person You want me to be. Amen."

Discussion Questions

1. What self-imposed pressures did Esther struggle with concerning sharing her faith?

2. What self-imposed pressures do you struggle with?

3. If we are self-driven, set out "to save" someone, or if we put our confidence in our best efforts, what is accomplished? Consider John 6:63.

4. What role did the Holy Spirit play in preparing Jim for salvation?

~

Obstacle Five: My Faith Seems Too Small.

"Yet, He saved them for His name's sake, to make His mighty power known"

(Psalm 106:8).

God does not require you to have great faith. You simply are to have faith in a great God. —Bill Bright

A Stubborn Father Gets Saved!

Richard Harris as told to Pamela Enderby

"If you have faith as small as a mustard seed ... Nothing will be impossible for you" (Matthew 17: 20).

Long before I entered kindergarten, Dad and I had become best buddies. He taught me how to identify a 9/16 wrench and how to eat peanuts the "correct way"— juggling them in my hand before popping them in my mouth. Right into adulthood I followed Dad like a shadow, barhopping and enjoying the "wild life."

When I turned 42 and received Christ as my Savior, the dynamics of our friendship drastically changed. A thick wedge grew between us.

Dad had always referred to God as the "big man upstairs." He believed the Lord wouldn't accept a drinking, cussing man like him. "But, Dad," I'd argue, "Jesus loves sinners."

He'd shut me off with a snarl, "I don't want to hear that stuff anymore."

Over the years my confidence in Dad's salvation frittered away. But my sister Marketta's unwavering faith kept her praying fervently and frequently. She even gave him a Bible when he turned 72.

Whenever Marketta talked about the day "Dad gets saved," my stomach would churn. I feared she was setting herself up for a huge disappointment. If Dad doesn't get saved, I thought, Marketta's faith might crumble. Worrying about my little sister's well-being drove me to dutiful witnessing.

At age 73, Dad moved into a trailer house on my property. As Dad sat underneath his carport, admiring the mysteries of nature, I'd often pull up a chair beside him and steer our conversation toward God. I'd share what God was doing in my life and what I had learned in church, but my stubborn father ignored me. My words seemed to float over his head. This guy will never get saved, I thought. I know Dad too well!

One day discouragement settled so deep in my heart that I resolved to quit witnessing. "Dad, I'm not going to bug you about this anymore. But, if you ever have questions about Jesus, you can always ask me." Then before I realized what I was saying, more words came tumbling out of my mouth, "Dad, if you get saved someday, I'm goin' to do some table dancing." Both of us chuckled.

Four months later, Dad's health failed drastically. Anemia and bone cancer fought to take his life, and he frequently received blood transfusions.

One evening, a nurse at the medical center phoned, "Rick, come down here. Your dad is not going to make it. It looks like it's all over." Immediately my thoughts turned toward Marketta. What will happen to her faith? I was filled with grief and despair for Dad and for Marketta.

My wife and I rushed to the hospital and found Dad lying awake flat on his back with his head slightly elevated.

Tubes wove their way in and out of his body, supporting his fragile life. He played tug of war with death.

"How are ya doing, Dad?" I whispered in his ear.

"I want to go home. I'm tired."

"You mean you want to go home to be with Jesus?" I asked, hopefully.

"Yes," he replied, squeezing my hand.

Encouraged by his answer, I quickly disowned my promise about never witnessing again. I could hardly ask the questions fast enough. "Do you know Jesus died on the cross? Do you know He died for your sins? Do you want to receive forgiveness for your sins?" To my amazement, he answered "yes" to all of them and then celebration broke loose.

Bursting into laughter, I climbed onto a small wood table in the hospital room and started dancing. Just then the nurse entered the room. Momentarily stunned, she listened to me explain the reason for my performance, and then she told me about my pastor visiting Dad that morning. He had led Dad through the prayer of salvation.

I could hardly wait to tell Marketta the good news; however, my announcement came as no surprise to her. "Rick," she said, matter-of-factly, "It only takes a little faith, mustard seed size, for God to change peoples' hearts." Her words exploded in my heart. Of course she was convinced of that, but I had given up on believing God would change Dad's heart. She was fully persuaded that God had power to do what He had promised. I believe her persistent faith-filled prayers softened Dad's heart to receive Christ as his Savior.

Dad miraculously lived through that turbulent night in the hospital. Then four days later, we celebrated his 75th birthday with cake and coffee. Shortly after, he returned home from the hospital and never needed another treatment. God had healed him both physically and spiritually.

Dad's love for God's Word grew and grew, and so did our talks about the Lord. Every evening we shared about

God's love and faithfulness. I never thought I'd see Dad radiate such peace.

Do you find it difficult sharing your faith with family members? Often our unbelieving moods, feelings, and emotions get in the way and we lose hope, viewing their lostness as greater than God's love. Don't lose heart. The miracles of the Bible do come alive today. With faith the size of a mustard seed, coupled with persevering prayer, God is in the business of saving even our most stubborn family member.

Discussion Questions

1. Hebrews 11:1 states, "Now faith is being sure of what we hope for and certain of what we do not see." Faith must be the foundation for successful outreach. Why?

2. When our faith is misplaced in our feelings, moods, and circumstances, how does it affect our witness?

3. Like Richard, you might know someone "too well" and think he/she will never get saved! What do the following salvation Scriptures promise?

Isaiah 59:1, Luke 19:10, 1 Timothy 1:15, Titus 3:5

4. Faith may be likened to a spiritual muscle. What happens when you exercise it? How will you exercise your outreach muscle?

5. Although Richard failed to persevere in prayer for his father's salvation, how did he reach out to his stubborn father? How may this encourage you to evangelize?

We are the womb of God upon the earth ... We do
not generate life, but we release, through prayer, Him
who does. —Dutch Sheets

Prayer Opens the Way for God to Do His Work

Pamela Enderby

"Devote yourselves to prayer ... that God may open a door
for our message" (Colossians 4:2).

I petitioned our small church. "Who will pray with me
for the lost?" Four outreach-minded members met with me
each Wednesday evening. For ten weeks we prayed by
name for our list of unbelieving family members, friends,
and neighbors. I anticipated an abundance of souls saved.
We prayed that:

1. God would open their spiritual eyes (2 Corinthians
4:4).

2. God would set them free from spiritual captivity (2
Timothy 2:25-26).

3. God would give them ears to hear (Matthew 13:15),
faith to believe (Acts 20:21), and the will to respond (Romans 10:9).

4. God would send people to witness to them (Matthew 9:38).

5. God would reveal ways to build caring relationships with them (1 Corinthians 9:22).

By the end of the prayer campaign, we knew of only one ten-year-old boy who had prayed to receive Christ. In my opinion, our outreach had failed. Perhaps we didn't pray hard enough, long enough, or with enough faith, I thought. As I expressed my disappointment to a friend, she cautioned me about trying to measure the effect of our prayers. "In God's perfect timing, He will save them," she encouraged me.

At church the following Sunday, my six-year-old daughter Anna begged me to follow her into the choir room to listen to her play the piano. When I entered the choir room, Anna had already found her place on the piano bench and was plunking on the keys with two teenage girls sitting beside her. I recognized the brunette sitting on Anna's right. Joy was a member of the youth group. She and her friend, sitting on Anna's left, acknowledged me with a smile.

After we exchanged friendly small talk, I assured Joy that the evangelistic prayer team had been praying for her unsaved friend. "What's her name?" I asked, in my absent-mindedness.

"Melissa," she grinned, pointing to the girl sitting on Anna's left.

Oh no, I thought. *I just called Melissa "unsaved." What if I offended her?* In my embarrassment, I wanted to slip out the door.

"Now, what do I say," I prayed, silently, then mustered up enough courage to speak.

"Melissa, did you enjoy church today?" It sounded like a reasonable question and one I had hoped she would respond to in a way that would give me enough time to think of something else to say. She nodded and smiled without a word.

"God, I feel helpless. You must come and help." I prayed again and waited, trusting God to give me His words. The silent seconds seemed like minutes.

Then a phrase that my Christian friend uses when he attempts to share his faith suddenly came to mind. "Melissa, do you know God or are you in the process of getting to know Him?" My words sounded amazingly smooth.

"I think I am getting to know Him," she replied.

My next question came with more boldness.

"Would you mind if I share some verses from the Bible that will help you know Him better?"

"Sure," she answered, still smiling.

The "Roman Road to Salvation" Scriptures I had once memorized escaped my mind. I grabbed my Bible and began searching its pages. Confusion kept me from recalling the first verse.

I sent another flash prayer. "God, please clear my mind. Help me remember where to begin."

Suddenly, Romans 3:23 came to mind. I read it out loud. "For all have sinned and fall short of the glory of God." After I explained it, Melissa agreed she was a sinner. Romans 6:23 followed easily. "For the wages of sin is death, but the gift of God is eternal life in Christ Jesus our Lord." My explanation of this verse coupled with Melissa's understanding of it led to Romans 10:9-10, the point of decision. "If you confess with your mouth that Jesus is Lord, and believe in your heart that God raised him from the dead, you will be saved. For it is with your heart that you believe and are justified, and it is with your mouth that you confess and are saved."

"Melissa, would you like to confess Jesus as your Savior?" As we bowed our heads, tears streamed down Joy's cheeks and mine, too. With heartfelt sincerity, Melissa repeated the words of my prayer that ushered her into God's kingdom. Joy's best friend and one more lost soul on my outreach list had just received Jesus.

The thrill of joining God in rescuing one more soul from hell's eternal flames compelled me to keep praying for the lost. I drove home from church rejoicing.

Two days later, I learned how Melissa put her new faith to work. A carload of kids, including Joy and Melissa, was hit by a train. After Melissa escaped the flaming wreckage, she realized Joy was still trapped. While crying out to God for help, she reentered the car and dragged Joy to safety.

Although Joy suffered third-degree burns and a collapsed lung, she survived the accident. I believe it took courage and Melissa's on the spot, faith-filled cries for help to save Joy's life.

Prayer is often tedious work, and hardly glamorous, but it's the essential part of God's plan for winning lost souls. Many times results are not immediate; however, prayer moves the hand of God. It woos, encourages, and loves the lost into a personal relationship with Him.

Isaiah 53:12 states that Jesus lives to make intercession for transgressors. He calls us, as His disciples, to do the same. What could please Him more? Our prayer campaign is over, but by God's grace, I will not retire from interceding for the lost. It opens the door for God to do His work.

Discussion Questions

1. First John 5:14-15 says, "This is the confidence we have in approaching God: that if we ask anything according to His will, he hears us. And if we know that he hears us—whatever we ask—we know that we have what we asked of him." Why should this promise fuel your faith for outreach prayers?

2. Questions that bridge a spiritual conversation are often difficult to ask. What question did Pamela use? Which of these questions do you feel most comfortable using?

What do you think is your purpose in life?

Do you believe there's a God? Why or why not?

If you were to die tonight, do you know whether you would go to heaven or hell?

Do you consider yourself a religious person?

How can a person find lasting peace in life and peace of mind?

Do you think God can be known in a personal way? May I share with you how I came to know God in a personal way?

3. Jesus lives to make intercession for transgressors. How might being involved in an outreach prayer campaign prepare your heart for evangelism?

4. Consider starting an evangelistic prayer campaign with a small group of outreach minded believers. Use the five prayer points outlined in the story.

Do all the good you can by all the means you can,
and in all the ways you can, and in all the places you
can, and at all the times you can, to all the people
you can, as long as you ever can. —John Wesley

The Winnebago Miracle

Ed Hamil as told to Pamela Enderby

"Now to him who is able to do immeasurably more than all
we ask or imagine" (Ephesians 3:20).

When I turned four months old, my raging, alcoholic father killed my mother and then committed suicide. A few days before my mother died, she told my grandmother, "I want you to take 'Little Eddy' if anything ever happens to me." My grandparents honored her request and adopted me into their loving arms.

In my teen years, I grew restless and began flirting with girls and going to wild parties with my buddies. It seemed senseless. I didn't want to ruin my life with drugs and alcohol, so I began questioning God about my purpose in life. Although He didn't give immediate answers to my questions, He faithfully led me on a journey to significant discoveries that unfolded my life's purpose.

My first discovery came when, as a nineteen-year-old, I accepted my friend's invitation to Bible study and was saved. After that I experienced a deep longing to share God's love with others. I often cried, "Lord, anoint me to help save the lost!"

I soon delved into a Sunday school class that offered training on how to witness using the Four Spiritual Laws booklet from Campus Crusade for Christ. Many believers today tell me that particular outreach approach is too mechanical for witnessing. Nevertheless, I discovered that God can use an available mouthpiece no matter how smooth or mechanical one sounds. Using that booklet led me to successful street witnessing.

By daily feeding on God's Word and memorizing Scriptures, I was building my own witnessing toolbox. It never ceased to amaze me how appropriate Scriptures, tucked in my memory bank, came to mind when I encountered a witnessing opportunity. Every outreach experience thrilled me; however, one in particular shines above the rest.

It started while I was attending Washburn University in Topeka, Kansas. While living on my deceased parents' social security income of $220 per month, I received a registered letter from a law firm stating that I was entitled to two pieces of oil property, one in Arkansas and one in Louisiana. I could hardly wait to scout out the land.

When college ended for summer break, I cruised out of Washburn in my '71 white Ford, drove four hundred miles, and arrived in Mena, Arkansas. The town stood dark and lifeless except for occasional midnight thunder crashes. Fear replaced my excitement. Gripping the steering wheel, with an empty gas tank and a few dollars in my pocket, I drove slowly ahead until I reached the edge of town. To my relief, I spotted a gas station with an adjoining café and motel. Observing the sleazy motel, I immediately put to practice what I had learned during my lean times—I began thanking God for His provisions.

The next morning, I again started the day by praising and praying a familiar prayer. "Lord, how can I show You my thanks? I'll do anything for You."

As I opened the bedroom shades, I saw a young man with long, stringy hair standing in the rain. He was extending a corner of his plastic poncho over his black lab. If he's going in my direction, I'll buy him breakfast at the café and give him a lift. We exchanged introductions and Jim, the hitchhiker, accepted my offer. After eating breakfast together, he corralled his smelly dog onto the back seat of my car and we drove off.

At that moment I experienced sheer bliss. I had a captive audience for using my favorite approach to share the Gospel. I call it the fisherman's approach. I throw out a Scripture, explain it, and wait for a response. If I sense enough interest, I throw out another Scripture.

After several miles of throwing out "bait" that aroused a lively discussion, I asked, "Jim, are you ready to make a decision? Do you want to ask Jesus into your heart to be your Lord and Savior?"

"No, I don't think so," he replied, hesitantly. Jim's response startled me because he had seemed extraordinarily hungry for the truth.

Usually I don't push the Gospel if I get resistance, but this time I felt compelled. "Jim, I don't want to sound pushy, but may I ask why you don't want to ask Jesus into your heart?"

"That's a fair question," he replied. "I've been hitchhiking for about six months, and I've met all kinds of people, even preachers. No one has been able to answer my question about people who worship Buddha and Krishna. How do I know for sure I shouldn't worship those gods?"

"Buddha and Krishna were mere men who are now dead," I replied. "My God is alive. He listens to our prayers and answers them. He knows everything about us and He's always here to help. As a matter of fact, He is able to do immeasurably more than all we ask or imagine!"

Jim remained silent. I continued, "Jim, if God proved to you that He is the only true, living God, would you give your life to Him?"

"Sure," he remarked, calmly.

At that moment, words began spilling out of my mouth before giving them much thought. "Jim, I believe God loves you. And I believe God would move a mountain for you if that's what it would take to get you saved. So I'm going to ask Him to do a miracle in your life in the next 24 hours. Then you'll know He is the only true God." Never before had I risked putting my faith on the line in such a way.

The whites of Jim's eyes grew large, like half moons. "Nothing bad will happen to you," I said, chuckling.

"Lord God," I prayed, "Would you please make Yourself real to Jim? Show him You are the only true God who loves him and came to earth to save him."

The traffic seemed unusually heavy that afternoon. Several cars passed us until we ended up trailing behind a Winnebago camper. Immediately I recognized words painted across its backside, but we were too far away to read them. Curiosity compelled me to accelerate until we could make out the words. When we were within a couple of yards, simultaneously, Jim and I read the string of four-inch block letters out loud. "Choose ye this day whom ye will serve, whether the Lord God of Israel or the gods of the heathen nations, but as for me and this household we will serve the Lord, Joshua 24:15."

Goosebumps covered my legs. The display of God's presence and power covering this camper left us speechless and stunned. I almost rear-ended it!

Jim was convinced. "I'm ready to pray with you," he said softly, bowing his head.

As Jim prayed, confessing Jesus as the only true God and Savior, tears streamed down my cheeks. It felt as though we were touching holy ground, even with his dog breathing down my neck!

130

In the New Testament, Jesus frequently tells His disciples to go and bear fruit in keeping with their salvation. So I suggested Jim do the same. He decided to return to Idaho and begin making things right with past relationships. He understood that his spiritual growth depended upon acts of repentance.

When we reached our departure point, we shook hands. Jim's beaming smile and the warmth of his spirit radiated the sincerity of his new life in Christ. I felt an indescribable joy watching him step forward, onto his new pathway of life. Who would have imagined God reaching out to a lost, searching soul from a Winnebago camper?

"Father, help me to remember that you are in the miracle-making business. You specialize in doing exceedingly, abundantly beyond what I can think or imagine! Please increase my faith that I might take more faith risks. Amen."

Discussion Questions

1. Ed discovered that witnessing gave purpose and meaning to his life. Do you agree or disagree? Why?

2. Ed took a faith risk by asking God to make Himself real to Jim. His prayer reflected Ephesians 3:20, "To Him who is able to do immeasurably more than all we ask or imagine, according to his power that is at work within us." Why should we take such faith risks?

3. Consider Jim's soul winning "fisherman's approach." What Scriptures could you use?

4. How might keeping a thankful heart attitude stimulate witnessing? Today, focus on the riches of God's blessings in your life. Consider making a "thankful list."

5. Ed's practice of memorizing and feeding on God's Word led to effective witnessing. Jesus states in John 14:25-26, "But the Counselor, the Holy Spirit, whom the Father will send in my name, will teach you all things and will remind you of everything I have said to you." Today, determine a time, a place, and a plan to cultivate personal study of God's Word.

The authority of Jesus Christ extends over all
creatures, whether human or superhuman.
—John Stott

Setting a Prisoner Free

Rob Conrad as told to Pamela Enderby

"You guided your people to make for yourself a glorious
name" (Isaiah 63:14).

The highlight of my week is visiting inmates at Johnson County jail although it's not a pretty sight. Scores of prisoners, speaking in loud voices, surrounded by vandalized cement walls, dusty ceilings, and wet floors, remain trapped. One new prisoner expressed his thoughts about jail life. "It's far from being mediocre at all. It's hell. It's suffocating."

I've never been incarcerated, but I know what living in bondage is like. Years ago, drugs and alcohol held me captive. They buried me in a state of worthlessness and emptiness. Then, one Sunday morning, my wife convinced me to attend church with her, and there, I met Jesus. His love has radically changed my life.

Today, one of my greatest joys is bringing freedom to prisoners by sharing God's message of grace and forgiveness. I see hearts' doors of some unlock, and they live free inside their prison cells.

One afternoon, I spotted a new inmate as a line of men trudged into a pod designated for Bible study. This Mexican American wore the familiar newcomer's hard, tough look with his baggy orange uniform. I reached for his hand and welcomed him. Except for his name, Fernando*, I could barely understand his broken English.

Fernando sat in the front row at Bible study. He eagerly accepted the Spanish Bible I offered him and also my help in pointing out Scriptures we were studying. Fernando's hunger for God's Word quickly became apparent as he voluntarily attended every meeting thereafter.

One afternoon following Bible study, Fernando drew me aside with his cellmate who spoke both Spanish and English. "I thought you were just some guy coming through the door trying to tell us what to do, but you really understand what we're going through." Then upon Fernando's request, his cellmate explained why Fernando had been arrested. He hitched a ride with a bunch of drug dealers traveling from Colorado to Kansas to search for a job. When the police stopped them to scour their car, they found it loaded with drugs. Unfortunately, Fernando was arrested and labeled the ringleader.

As I listened to the details of Fernando's arrest, sadness filled his eyes. He pulled from his pocket a worn picture of his wife and three kids. They, too, reflected hopelessness and desperation.

For two months Fernando remained in jail pending adjudication. Meanwhile, I often guided him to Jesus' words in his Spanish Bible. "The truth will set you free" (John 8:32). Sometimes doubt veiled his faith and mine, too. I'd turn to God's Word for encouragement and share it with Fernando through his Spanish-speaking cellmate. "God knows the situation; He knows the truth. He will let the judge know the truth, too."

Just before Fernando's court date arrived, he slipped me a note requesting that I attend his hearing. Anxiety gnawed at him like a bird pecking its prey. He needed a friend.

"I'll be there," I promised.

The day of the trial, Fernando's mother, wife, and children crouched beside him on the wooden bench. Without speaking a word, I waved for his attention and offered him one last boost of encouragement. Folding my hands prayerfully, I pointed heavenward, and mouthed the words, "Pray, 'The truth will set you free.'"

To be honest, I wanted to believe Fernando would be set free, but I was skeptical. This Spanish-speaking convict hardly stood a chance against the law that was stacked against him.

I settled back into my seat and immediately pleaded, "Oh, Lord Jesus, please step in because Your reputation is at stake here." When I looked up, I saw an unusually large number of police officers leaning against the courtroom wall. I felt as though someone had just kicked me in the stomach. "Lord, please set Fernando free," I begged again. "He needs to experience Your love and mercy. I've been telling him how personal You are and that You care for him."

As the seemingly hopeless case unfolded, God showcased His power and authority. To begin, Fernando's public defendant picked the police apart for doing an illegal search and false arrest. When the jury finally voted, they declared Fernando, "Not guilty."

Fernando glanced at me, his eyes grew wide with excitement, and he gave me the thumbs up signal. I rejoiced. "Thanks, God, for pulling us through this!"

Although Fernando's case was dismissed, he was ordered to remain in jail a few more days to give the prosecutors opportunity to appeal. When Fernando requested a private visit with me, God showed up a second time.

The guards guided me to a cracker-box sized room on the jail's second floor. A heavy metal door locked behind me as I entered.

When Fernando walked in and saw me waiting for him behind the window, he started weeping. "You were right! You were right!" he cried. "I want your Jesus." I could barely understand his words, except for "Jesus."

I was keenly aware of the huge language barrier I was facing, but I didn't give in to it. God had already proven His power in the courtroom, inspiring me to press on. I felt compelled to share the Gospel in English as simply as possible. When I began praying out loud for Fernando, the Lord's presence and power filled the jail cell. A revival of joy exploded, filling Fernando's countenance, and both of us wept tears of joy.

The Apostle Paul's testimony rang true in my heart. "I came to you in weakness, timid, and trembling. And my message and my preaching were very plain. I did not use wise and persuasive speeches, but the Holy Spirit was powerful among you. I did this so that you must trust the power of God rather than human wisdom" (I Corinthians 2:3 NLT).

Had Fernando received Christ into his heart? Two days later, I found out for sure.

At Bible study, Fernando greeted me with a warm hug. His face still glowing.

"Is Fernando really free?" his cellmate asked, curiously.

I assured him the judge had pronounced Fernando innocent. "Ask Fernando what I prayed with him the other day when he said, 'I want your Jesus.'"

Listening to the cellmate relate Fernando's response, I stood speechless. He echoed the same simple Gospel presentation I had shared with Fernando, word for word. God's indescribable power had broken through what looked like an impossible situation, a language barrier. Without a doubt, He translated my prayer and the Gospel into Fernando's language!

Ordinary people like me are making a difference in prisoners' lives. I feel honored and humbled to be one of His vessels. Often it takes several visits of sharing my life with them and taking time to listen to what's on their hearts before I might gain their confidence, but once their trust levels grow, and they view me as authentic and understanding, their hearts turn soft and fertile to receive the truth.

*name changed

Discussion Questions

1. In this story and throughout the Bible, God demonstrates His supernatural power setting captives free. He proves, "He is the Lord God." Read of Elijah's showdown with Baal's prophets in 1 Kings 18:20-40. What happened? What other examples of "signs, wonders, and miracles" in the Bible precipitated revival?

2. In Matthew 28:18-19 Jesus commands us: "Go with my power." It has been stated, "God doesn't call the equipped. He equips the called." How did God equip Rob?

3. What impossible situation are you facing with an unbeliever today that requires a miracle?

4. Hebrews 13:3 states, "Remember those in prison as if you were their fellow prisoners." Do you sense God leading you to visit the incarcerated or write a prisoner? If so, contact: Prison Fellowship, P.O. Box 17500, Washington, DC 20041-0500; Tel/703-478-0100; www.pfm.org

5. Consider praying for a prisoner. Craig F. Stevenson, an inmate in Soledad, California, invites us to pray Colossians 1:3-29 on behalf of the incarcerated.

We need love's tender lessons taught as only weakness can; God has his small interpreters; the child must teach the man. —John Greenleaf Whittier

Humpty Dumpty to King Jesus

Pamela Enderby

"Let the little children come to me, and do not hinder them" (Mark 10:14).

Anna bolted through our front door, breathless, calling, "Mom, where are you?" I quickly pushed aside the mail I was reading and headed for the door. Usually I welcomed her home from school with a warm hug, but that day she resisted my embrace and plopped down on the couch, excited.

"Mom, listen to this." She yanked her backpack off and unfolded a piece of notebook paper. "I wrote down everything Haley* told me at school today so I wouldn't forget." Anxiously she reported, "Haley had a dream about the devil last night. He told her he loved her and would give her anything she wanted if she'd follow him." She breathed another heavy sigh. "Mommm ... What are we going to do?"

Haley's face, the obstinate first grader I had dreaded working with last year, came to my mind. Haley snubbed my help and questioned my authority as a volunteer teacher's aid. And since she didn't hang out with well-behaved, well-mannered kids, I preferred Anna to keep her distance from Haley.

"I told Haley the devil is bad and that he hates her," Anna continued. "And I told her the devil is lying to her and that he really wants to hurt her." Again, she pleaded, "Mom … What are we going to do?"

Until then, I had not given much thought to Anna's un-saved public school friends. They seemed harmless, for the most part. However, this incident triggered a couple of daunting questions. Do we get involved with this spiritually misguided eight-year-old? If we do, will her evil influence corrode Anna's faith?

"Let's pray for her," I said, hoping that would appease Anna and put the situation to rest. But my safe, unspoken, "Let's keep our distance" preference wouldn't satisfy her.

"We can pray, Mom, but we have to buy her a Bible. Can we go to the store right now?" I reluctantly acquiesced. It meant delaying dinner preparations and also my list of phone calls. I hid my impatience and calmly agreed. "Let's go."

That evening Anna wrote a note in Haley's new Bible. "Dear Haley, Jesus loves you. Your friend, Anna." I didn't know how Anna's teacher would feel about her handing out a Bible at school, so I wrapped it in tissue paper. "Tell Haley to open it when she gets home," I instructed. The following day, Anna proudly marched into school with her treasure tucked under her arm.

At bedtimes we continued to discuss Haley's spiritual outlook and asked Jesus to protect her from the devil and bring her to salvation. The more I prayed, I began imagining this blue-eyed, helpless child with blond braided pig-tails trapped in the devil's clutches, crying for help. My attitude toward Haley slowly changed from indifference to heartfelt concern, and my faith for her salvation grew steadily.

A couple of weeks later, Anna asked if Haley could play at our house. By that time I had warmed up to the possibility of Anna befriending Haley.

Haley and Anna enjoyed a full afternoon of jumping on the trampoline and playing dolls. Their time spent together went so well, that she accepted Anna's invitation to go to church with her the following Sunday.

Haley was waiting on her porch step as we pulled into her driveway early Sunday morning. I learned that Haley knew very little about God and that she had only attended church once before for her cousin's baptism.

That morning, our guest worship leader sang an unusual and creative song about "Humpty Dumpty." He was empty hearted and full of cracks, but King Jesus valiantly rescued him and succeeded at making him whole. After the song, instead of following the rest of the kids to children's church, Haley approached my side with questioning eyes. I bent down and whispered in her ear, "What's wrong?" She whispered back, "I feel empty in my heart, too, just like that man was talking about. I want it to go away. What should I do?" Her eyes searched mine.

Overhearing Haley's question, Anna's face lit up. "Let's go over there," I said to the girls, pointing to a sunny, quiet spot at the back of the church. Then, with my encouragement, Anna shared the Good News with Haley in a delightfully natural and unpretentious way,

"Do you want to ask Jesus into your heart now?" Anna asked.

We held hands while Haley sincerely repeated the prayer of salvation, following Anna's words. Lifting her head, she said, "Katie needs Jesus, too. Katie thinks devils are good." At that moment, Haley and Anna agreed to pray for Katie, their third-grade classmate.

On the way home, Haley cheerfully announced her new found revelation, "When I die, I'm not going to hell; I'm going to heaven!" Then with her eyes twinkling, she softly whispered, "Is it all right to say 'hell'?" Anna and I burst into laughter.

It's no wonder Jesus said, "Let the little children come to me, and do not hinder them, for the kingdom of God belongs to such as these" (Mark 10:14). God knows our children's extraordinary potential. Through them He is willing to execute His plans to extend His kingdom. The question I must ask myself is, "Will I let Him?"

* name changed

Discussion Questions

1. Why did Pamela initially want to discourage Anna from building a friendship with Haley? How do you feel about your child(ren) building relationships with unchurched or unsaved kids?

2. What steps did Anna and Pamela take to minister to Haley without compromising their values or putting Anna in spiritual danger?

3. How was Pamela's faith affected by this outreach?

4. Sometimes parenting our own children seems to be an overwhelming task. To extend care to other youngsters requires supernatural stamina. Consider ways God can assist you in helping your children evangelize. Which of the following might fit your family?

Give to the poor. Help your child identify a needy child at school or in the neighborhood. Teach your child the importance of giving by setting aside some of her allowances. After a few months, combine her savings with your contributions. Go shopping together and then let your child anonymously leave the items on the doorstep.

Prayer releases power. Collect pictures of unsaved classmates and neighbor kids. Post them in an album, one to a page. At bedtime, let your child select a picture and pray together for that child.

Plan a party. Holidays offer timely opportunities to invite your kids' friends into your home to play Christ-centered games. Get your kids involved in writing party invitations, preparing snacks, and selecting game ideas.

Play praise music. While transporting kids to social events, play upbeat praise tapes; often clapping and singing will naturally flow. This primes questions and conversation about Jesus.

Hide and seek. Collect wicker baskets from thrift stores or garage sales. After your child decorates them with colorful tissue paper, add homemade cookies and attach a tag that says, "Jesus loves you." One at a time, your child drops a basket on their friends' doorstep, rings the doorbell, and runs. The suspense of not "getting caught" fuels this activity.

Encourage your kids to share their stories. Personal testimonies illustrate God's "realness." One day, I overheard Anna tell her friend that God answered her older sister's prayer by giving her a baby sister.

~

Obstacle Six: I've Never Received Evangelism Training.

"This is the victory that has overcome the world, even our faith."

(1 John 5:4)

Every Christian can tell his or her story. We can share out of our own experience what God has done in our lives. —Leighton Ford

A Priest Gets Saved

John Enderby as told to Pamela Enderby

"O Lord, I have never been eloquent ... I am slow of speech and tongue'" (Exodus 4:10).

"How does a person get to heaven?"

As I carefully listened to seventh and eighth grade boys in my Sunday School class give their answers, I felt inclined to pass out a homework assignment. Each student was to contact a church leader from various denominations, such as Lutheran, Methodist, Catholic, Baptist, Presbyterian, or Nazarene and ask, "How does a person get to heaven?" The following Sunday they would report their findings.

My personal spiritual journey fueled this assignment. Just one year earlier, I had converted to Catholicism in order to marry my wife. While attending St. Anthony's membership classes, I learned that by receiving the sacraments of baptism and confirmation and by going to confession and church regularly, I would secure my place in heaven.

Practicing these religious rules, though, left my wife and me spiritually empty.

As newlyweds, we moved to a small factory town in Mosinee, Wisconsin and met a State Farm insurance agent and his wife, also newly married. They pursued our friendship by inviting us to dinner and sporting events. As they gained our trust, we eventually shared our marital conflicts. Fortunately, they encouraged and counseled us as best they knew how, but more importantly, they committed to pray for us. Then one Saturday afternoon at a football game, they popped the question. "Do you want to go to church with us this Sunday?" We agreed, feeling obligated to the friendship.

The church was filled with farm families and the smell of cow manure wafted through the windows. It upset my stomach. I could hardly wait until the service was over.

A few days later, the telephone rang. "Hi, this is Pastor Andy from Stratford Community Bible Church. Would it be all right if I paid you a visit tonight?" I reluctantly agreed.

That evening Pastor Andy shared stories about his hippie drug-taking days in the '60s. He had even threatened his wife with a knife. What kind of a preacher is this guy? After he explained how God had changed his life and saved his marriage, my suspicions dissolved. It was the first time in my 24 years I had heard the true salvation message: Eternal life comes by trusting in Christ's finished work on the cross, not by doing good works. That evening, on November 17, 1974, Pastor Andy led my wife and me through the sinner's prayer.

After our conversion, God not only began to mend our marriage, but He also created a gnawing hunger in me to share the Good News with others, especially those who put their trust in religious, man-made rules for salvation as I once did. Since I never had the opportunity to take evangelism training after I got saved, I simply relied on sharing my salvation story to be enough.

Now, pondering God's grace and mercy working in my life, I, too, delved into the Sunday school assignment. First thing Monday morning I picked up the phone to call St. Dominic's Parish in Sheboygan, Wisconsin.

Waiting for someone to answer the phone, I rehearsed my question. "I need your help with a Sunday School assignment. Do you mind if I ask you some questions?"

A friendly voice at the other end of the line interrupted my thoughts. "Father George* speaking."

I introduced myself, then blurted my question. At first Father George echoed similar doctrinal answers I had heard in premarital membership classes. Then he cracked the door open to allow me to see his heart. "But I'm not so sure I agree with these teachings," Father George said, hesitantly. "In fact," he added, "I have a few questions of my own."

Leaning back in my swivel chair, I glanced down at my open Bible. Jesus' words seemed to jump out. "I will make you fishers of men." At that moment, I felt certain this well-meaning priest was one hungry fish searching for spiritual food and that God intended I catch him.

After exchanging small talk, I asked, "Father George, do you mind if I give you a copy of the New Testament?"

"Fine," he said, "Drop it off at the school." The next day, I stopped by the parochial school where Father George taught. He accepted not only the Bible, but also my invitation to have dinner with my wife and me.

Father George arrived for dinner dressed in traditional priest's garb: black pants and a white, short-sleeved shirt overlaying his stiff priest's collar. When we were comfortably seated at our dining room table, I began to unfold my list of questions. "So, why did you become a priest?"

"I grew up in a large family with ten siblings and hardly got enough to eat. But the priests, they're a different story," he laughed, heartily. "I knew they always had enough food on their tables. So I figured the priesthood would be a good job."

I thought he was joking. He didn't say anything about God calling him to the priesthood.

I had heard enough. I was convinced this priest needed to know Jesus as Savior and develop a personal relationship with Him.

After dinner, in the comfort of our living room, Father George volunteered more information. He began, proudly, "When I became a priest I vowed to read from a devotional book everyday. And I've honored my vow." He hung his head and paused, "But sometimes I drink too much and then I feel like a hypocrite."

I'm not sure if I felt sorry for him or embarrassed, but before I could offer a consoling word, he interrupted my thoughts by recounting a few of his recent good deeds. He was striving to regain my respect, his eyes searching mine for approval throughout his narrative.

Father George's best efforts to hide his shame fueled my desire even more to give him the truth. I remembered how guilty and shameful I used to feel no matter how much good I did, trying to offset the bad.

"Father George," I said, "May I share my spiritual journey with you?" He leaned into the couch and nodded. "The first 24 years of my life, I lived to please myself by drinking and chasing after women. I also believed making money would make me happy. All of that left me feeling guilty and empty inside, so I tried doing more good than bad. Still, I always ended up feeling more unworthy."

Pointing to my open Bible, I said, "But now I know better. I have good news to share." As I read some Scriptures from the book of Romans, Father George listened intently, motionless. I explained how God came to forgive and save sinners like me. I could sense the Holy Spirit working.

"Even Martin Luther couldn't satisfy the church's man-made rules! He was tormented by guilt and felt dead inside trying to live up to them." I figured Father George had studied Luther in seminary and would identify with him.

Father George bent forward in his chair, clutched the open Bible I handed him, and cleared his throat, "That sounds like me."

"You don't have to earn your salvation," I continued. "Just like Luther, you can be free from the bondage of works, trying to earn God's approval. All you have to do is receive God's unconditional love and forgiveness."

He still didn't get it. He restated his past priestly acts of service, precisely and slowly, as if they had the power to pardon his sins. Then I gently reminded him. "We're all sinners in need of a Savior, Father George, no matter how many good works we do. Trusting in Christ's work on the cross is the only way the penalty for our sins is paid."

Realizing the need to review the Scriptures I had read earlier, I asked him to turn to Romans 3:23. After he fumbled through the pages of the New Testament, he found his place. Carefully, I explained Romans 3:23, then Romans 6:23 and Romans 5:8. Then I led him to Ephesians 2:8-9 and asked him to read.

"You see, Father George. Salvation is a free gift. It's called God's grace." I paused and then asked, "Do you want to receive this free gift?"

His spiritual eyes had opened. On that cool spring evening, with Father George's consent, we got on our knees. Fifteen years had passed since he entered the priesthood, dedicating himself to serving God. In seminary he had routinely been told to pray the Hail Mary or the Our Father to temporarily clear his conscience. This time was different. Father George prayed from his heart and a new life emerged.

Before Father George left that evening, I reinforced that salvation is a free gift and read from Ephesians 2:8-9 (TLB). "It's by God's grace that you have been saved through faith. It's not the result of your own efforts, but God's gift, so that no one can boast about it."

The following week, I returned to my Sunday school class eager to share Father George's salvation experience.

Many of my students also interviewed church leaders who believed in salvation based upon good works. Our discoveries gave us an even greater appreciation for God's mercy and grace working in our lives, and for some, it was the first time their eyes and hearts were opened to lost "religious" people who need to receive eternal life through faith in Jesus Christ.

I wonder how many "religious" people we come in contact with in our churches who have missed out on receiving the wonderful, free gift of God's unconditional love and forgiveness.

*name changed

Discussion Questions

1. In Acts 10:2 Cornelius is a good example of a "religious" person. How does Scripture describe him?

2. Cornelius already worshipped the true God (Acts 10:36), but according to Acts 11:14-15, what did Cornelius and his household need to receive from God?

3. Elisabeth Elliot suggests, "If someone says they are a Christian, ask them, 'What did you receive when you became a Christian?'" Why is this a good question?

4. John had not received evangelism training, but God still used him to tell his salvation story. Why was it effective? Note how he began and how he ended. Practice telling your story, keeping it within three minutes.

5. If we're yielded to God, our lives become roads He travels touching, rescuing, and redeeming lives. Begin praying for the "Cornelius" that may attend your church, Bible study, or small group. How might you reach out to that person?

Make me a blessing, make me a blessing. Out of my
life may Jesus shine. —Ira B. Wilson

A Bus Driver Shows Compassion

Marty Vierra as told to Pamela Enderby

"You are the light of the world ... let your light shine before
men" (Matthew 5:14).

A sudden sheet of rain swept across my windshield. I drove slowly, practically crawling down the country road headed for Jane and Jimmy's dilapidated house. Usually they stood outside waiting for me, dressed in soiled pants and shirts, but today no one appeared. I snaked the school bus into their driveway and beeped the horn.

The bus shook as thunder rumbled and lightning ripped through the sky. I pulled closer and beeped again. No response. Panic swept over me.

I shoved the stick shift into park, turned my flashers on, and peered into my rearview mirror. "Megan," I called. "Do you think you can keep these kids quiet for a few minutes? I think Jimmy and Jane are in trouble."

"Sure," she exclaimed, confidently. Megan was the oldest and most responsible child on the bus.

When I ran across the driveway to the backdoor, a crack of lightning split the sky and zapped an oak tree in the yard. It sent a shock wave through me that made my skin tingle. When I opened the back door natural gas fumes hit me in the face. I took a deep breath, held it, and quickly stepped into the cramped, dreary quarters. The whole family was asleep on the living room floor. I tried to shake them awake.

"I'm here to take the kids to school." I said in a loud voice.

At first, no one responded. I opened a window and kept shaking the kids until finally, to my relief, the whole family roused.

"Notify your landlord right away that you have a gas leak," I said to the parents. "I'll help the kids get dressed for school."

Rushing out the door with their hair uncombed and teeth unbrushed, the children ducked their heads against the pelting rain. Relief swept over me when we reached the bus. Everyone was safe.

When I finished my route that morning, I reported Jane and Jimmy's poor living conditions to the school principal. He graciously overlooked my tardiness and informed the proper authorities. Later I learned the children were put in foster homes. It was sad to think I'd never see them again; however, God had a different plan.

Three years later, I was assigned to drive a busload of fourth graders to a children's museum. While watching the kids enjoy new discoveries, I felt a soft tapping on my leg. I turned around. Jane, now tall and gangly, stood staring at me. When she caught full view of me, she grabbed my hand and squeezed it tightly.

"Marty, Marty, is it really you?"

I pulled her close. Tears sparkled in her eyes.

151

"Jane, it's so good to see you," I said, giving her a big hug. "How is your brother?" While we chatted, Jane's fondness for me danced in her eyes, a reward I will never forget.

While driving a bus the next ten years, God has allowed me to evangelize more kids than I had ever dreamed. Everyday, I draw on His grace when little ones shuffle into my bus, and I draw deeply on His enabling power and energy to accomplish His purposes. I hand them crayons and pictures to color, and then when they finish their "masterpieces," I proudly post them above the bus windows. I love watching their self-esteem soar. For birthdays I dole out pencils engraved with a Scripture and give them certificates that say, "You're One of a Kind."

Evangelizing with God's kindness also includes His discipline. If the kids get too rowdy, I speak to them directly and firmly, insisting they quiet down. They thrive on respect and attention.

Bus driving is undoubtedly making a difference for God's kingdom, and it's changing my life as well. When I sleep I dream of children's lost souls; when I awake they are first in my thoughts. I never imagined driving a school bus could change so many lives, including mine!

Discussion Questions

1. In Matthew 5:14-16, Jesus calls us "the light of the world." According to these verses, when are we most effective as light?

2. When are we least effective?

3. "Shiny Christians" make effective evangelists. What are some keys to being "shiny" Christians?

Psalm 34:5

Daniel 12:3

2 Corinthians 3:18

Philippians 2:14-16

4. Marty could have jeopardized his job when he put Megan in charge. What risk(s) are you taking to let your "light shine?"

5. Marty did the work of an evangelist although he never received evangelism training. By studying and applying the following Scriptures, how can you, too, do the work of an evangelist? 1 Corinthians 3:6-7; Ephesians 6:10-12, 18; James 1:5; Acts 4:29; 2 Timothy 1:7-8; 2:1; 2 Timothy 2:23-26; 4:2, 5.

God doesn't force us into service. He invites us. And
when we make ourselves available to him, watch out!
He will take us up on our offer. —David J. Deters

Throw a Block Party

Pamela Enderby

"I will cause my people and their homes around my holy
hill to be a blessing" (Ezekiel 34:26 TLB).

Year after year, I tried various approaches to build
friendships with my neighbors. During the warm months, I
stopped to chat with my neighbors while taking walks or
while gardening. On May Day, Valentine's Day, and
Christmas, my children and I delivered homemade cookies
with generous doses of cheer. One New Year's Day, I invited my neighbors in for wassail and light snacks. Of
course, all these evangelistic efforts and others helped cultivate friendships, but I had not seen or heard evidence of
any spiritual transformations. Since I had run out of practical outreach ideas coupled with feeling like a failure, I figured I wasn't cut out for evangelism.

That's when I talked with a friend who had hosted a
neighborhood block party. She said she had grown closer to
her neighbors in one afternoon than in the entire ten years

she had lived there. Listening to her experience infused me with fresh excitement to try again.

Planning my party began with prayer. I didn't know what else to do, so with a neighborhood directory in hand, I prayed frequently for my neighbors during my quiet times. When my husband John and I took evening walks around the neighborhood, we sensed common spiritual strongholds such as materialism and isolation. "Lord," we prayed, "break the barriers between our neighbors and help us love one another." Using the "BLESSing" acronym* from *Developing a Prayer-Care-Share Lifestyle* by Dr. Alvin J. Vander Griend also helped guide our prayers.

On the heels of summer, my schedule grew busier with kids' activities, and my confidence in being effective at evangelism wavered. But God encouraged me to press on every time I offered Him my anxieties. Thoughts of failure haunted me, such as, *What if only a few people come? What if no one talks with each other? What if this party is a flop?* So, I pleaded, "Lord, please make this block party a lot of fun!"

One day I decided to recruit help from Ted, my elderly neighbor with whom I'd grown acquainted by striking up conversations with him as he worked in his yard. Ted loved fishing for neighborhood "gossip," so this event was an attractive opportunity to him!

During the next few weeks, John and I continued our evening walks and stopped to chat with our neighbors about the block party. This set the stage for Ted's hand delivered invitations, colorful flyers that included the party's time, date, and location. The invitations requested guests bring their own meat to bar-be-cue, along with a dish to pass. RSVPs were directed to Ted.

When the big day arrived, the aroma of burning charcoal met me as I hurried to the empty lot beside Ted's house. Ted had proudly set up a food table covered with a bright yellow canopy. Unloading my party supplies, brats, and beans on the table, I silently repeated my familiar plea, "Oh, Lord, please help us have fun."

When my neighbors arrived, they wrote their names on large nametags. Now, ready or not, all eyes were on me. With my heart beating wildly and my stomach squirming, I shouted, "Time to play games."

First, I divided the group into two teams, red versus blue, and gave three yo yos to each team. The team that could "yo yo" the longest won first prize. We played several more team games, with the whistling contest stirring the most laughs. The player who chewed and swallowed two dry crackers, then whistled "Yankee Doodle" first won a prize.

When we finally arranged our lawn chairs in a circle and sat down to eat, everyone appeared relaxed and friendly, and I silently thanked God for making the party a success.

By mid afternoon, the sun had grown hotter, and I figured it was time to wrap up the party. Just then, I heard a car horn blaring. Whirling around, I faced the busy street behind Ted's house and saw a young man hanging his head out the window of his bright red Chevy Camero. He yelled, "Hey! What's going on over there?"

"We're having a party and you're invited!" my husband called back, motioning him. The man waved and sped off. I assumed I wouldn't see him again.

Moments later, the fancy red sports car pulled up to the street curb near our party and the young man climbed out. "Hi, I'm Brian," he said with a grin as he strolled across the freshly cut green grass toward us. "Thanks for inviting me!"

Immediately, my neighbors greeted him with smiles and handshakes. After savoring a huge helping of picnic food, Brian pulled a deck of cards from his pocket. "May I show you a few tricks?" My neighbors' applause and whistles cheered him on to perform clever card tricks interspersed with funny, clean jokes. He captured our attention for the rest of the afternoon.

"Did you hire this guy?" My neighbors asked. "He's fantastic!"

"I've never seen him before," I replied. "I have no idea where he's from."

When Brian finally introduced himself as a professional improvisator, I looked him in the eye and queried. "You mean you're really a professional comedian?"

"Yeah," he replied, matter-of-factly. "I work at a comedy club. I love to act and make people laugh."

At that moment, I realized the depth of God's faithfulness. He had answered my prayer beyond what I had asked for! He provided our own private comedy show! He sent Brian, a professional comedian, to add "a lot of fun" to our block party!

The next day, I saw my next-door neighbor Darlene working in her garden, pulling dead blooms off her petunias. She waved to me, smiling.

"What a terrific block party! We've lived here for fifteen years, and I've never felt as close to my neighbors as I do now," she said.

I agreed. God's favor rested upon my neighborhood in an unusual way that afternoon. His storehouse of blessings came perfectly timed with fun-filled entertainment, sunny skies, and a backyard full of neighbors eagerly wanting to "party." Listening to my neighbors' belly laughs and watching their warm interactions were my greatest reward that day.

I don't need evangelism training when God gets involved in my neighborhood because there's no telling what He's going to do. But, one thing is certain: There will be "a lot of fun" because He is an expert party planner!

* Prayer walking helps bring about effective neighborhood evangelism. Consider prayer walking your neighborhood today, using the following "BLESSing" acronym from *Developing a Prayer-Care-Share Lifestyle*, by Hope

Ministries, ministry of Harvest Prayer Ministries. This resource can be ordered from HOPE Ministries: 800-217-5200 or online: www.harvestprayer.com

Body. Pray they may look to God who is prepared to "give them their food at the proper time" (Psalm 145:15).

Labor. Pray that they may keep their lives "free from the love of money and be content with what they have" (Hebrews 13:5).

Emotional. Pray that they may have "the unfading beauty of a gentle and quiet spirit, which is of great worth in God's sight" (1 Peter 3:4).

Social. Pray that they will "bear with each other and forgive whatever grievances [they] may have against one another" (Colossians 3:13).

Spiritual. Pray that they may confess Jesus as Lord, believe God raised Him from the dead, and be saved (Romans 10:9).

Be open to impressions and burdens of the Holy Spirit and pray as He leads you.

Block parties bridge friendships quickly. Although a professional improvisator may not show up at your neighborhood party, whether it's an apartment complex, condominium, or house, consider playing these games to promote "a lot of fun."

1. Each player receives a hula-hoop. See who can "hula" the longest before the hoop falls to the ground.

2. Ask for two men and two women volunteers. The men hold the end of an inflated balloon between their teeth while the women cover the balloon with shaving cream. The first woman who shaves the balloon without popping it wins.

3. Everyone receives a piece of bubble gum. Who can blow the biggest bubble?

4. Give each player a knotted rope and gloves. Whoever unties all the knots first wins.

5. One person from each team juggles three balls. Who can juggle the longest without dropping the balls?

6. Give each player a raw egg. Toss it back and forth, moving farther apart with each throw until the egg drops. Keep a bucket of water handy for clean up!

Discussion Questions

1. Prayer walking is an important first step in neighborhood evangelism. Explain why.

2. After months and years of building neighborhood friendships, Pamela still saw little results. Although she felt discouraged and ready to quit evangelizing, how do you think those contacts helped the block party be a success?

3. At the block party, no one said anything spiritual. Does that mean the party was an evangelistic failure? Why or why not?

4. Exercising your evangelistic muscle means cultivating common interests with your neighbors. Make a list of possible common contact points. For example: golf, walking, jogging, biking, gardening.

*Though God uses men as means for achieving His
purposes, in the last analysis nothing depends on
man; everything depends, rather, on the God who
raises men up to do His will. —J. I. Packer*

Like a Gentle Shepherd
He Leads Us

Sue Prosch as told to Pamela Enderby

*"God loved us and chose us in Christ to be holy and
without fault in his eyes" (Ephesians 1:4 TLB).*

I suspected God was up to something big. Fifteen years
had passed since Lisa and I had contact. Now, on the phone
and sobbing, she explained that a piece of paper with my
phone number scribbled on it had fallen out of her billfold.
Moments earlier she had cried out, "Oh, God, is there
someone I can talk with?"

During our college years, Lisa kept her painful childhood memories a secret. She was repeatedly used as a pawn
in her parent's power struggle. When they finally decided
to divorce, they battled more fiercely, each one trying to
make Lisa take his or her side. As a young woman, Lisa's
insecurities and deep-seated fears intensified and drove her

to see a psychiatrist. Her doctor insisted she receive shock treatments, as her condition grew worse. The treatments left this lonely, young mother more confused and hopeless until her emotional pain nearly paralyzed her.

Four months after Lisa called, she and her husband Bill came to Birmingham, Alabama, to visit relatives and me. I invited Lisa to a Bible study, but she resisted because she heard rumors that I had turned into a religious fanatic and was involved in something "weird." I felt somewhat offended, but Jesus' gentle reminder kept persisting, "Love her as I have loved you."

With a small amount of coaxing, Lisa decided to come. Attending Bible study put her on a healing path. Using Lisa's words, she had "wonderfully weird" experiences worshipping God and studying the Word.

When she returned home, she called me, "Sue, something incredible happened to me when we were attending Bible study. For three days, now, I've felt peaceful!" For the first time, I heard life and hope in Lisa's voice. She had tasted her first morsel of freedom.

With her fears about me laid aside, Lisa called frequently. I spoke God's Word to her emotional issues, but her mind struggled to sustain the truth. Under her doctor's guidance, she continued shock treatments while I carried her in prayer.

Six months later marked another turning point when Lisa and Bill returned to Birmingham for their second visit. The summer evening they arrived torrents of rain flashed across the city, but Lisa still insisted on seeing me. A deep mystery was about to unfold.

No sooner had I hung up than the phone rang again. "Bill doesn't want me driving in this storm. But, I feel so strongly that I'm supposed to see you tonight. What should I do?" Lisa asked, exasperated.

Again, recognizing God in this, I encouraged her. "Promise Bill you'll be very careful. I'll be praying he lets you come."

When Lisa arrived at my door that stormy evening, I greeted her with a hug and showed her into my kitchen. She slumped into a chair without speaking a word. Strangely, I, too, felt compelled to silence.

As the moonlight cracked through the curtains, I felt the presence of the Lord hovering over us like a blanket. It seemed we sat in holy silence for a long time. Finally Lisa began sobbing. Although she's a very private person, she cried out to God for help, weeping and agonizing over her emotional bondage.

At that moment, I was certain God didn't need my help. I just pressed Kleenex in her hand, one after another, patted her shoulder and remained silent. Most of the evening, Lisa spent sobbing and lamenting over past hurts. God's powerful love was reaching in, touching her deepest wounds. He was providing a cleansing and healing her heart to prepare her to receive Him.

Finally, words began forming in my mind. "Lisa, God never rejects a broken and contrite heart," I whispered. "He looks at you through all the love that prompted him to go to Calvary. He's calling, 'My child, I love you. I have loved you since before you were born. Come and enter my kingdom.'"

Finally, Lisa fell limp. I placed her hand in mine and invited her to let God take her burdens once and for all. She half smiled and faintly squeezed my hand. As she talked to God with childlike faith, unloading more pain, her face seemed to take on the appearance of an angel, peaceful and radiant. My soul was rejoicing in the birth of a new life.

God drew Lisa to faith in Christ by His sovereignty in grace, not at her own whim. I had never seen anyone more prepared to meet Christ. If I had predicted the time and details of her salvation, I would have failed. God's ways are far beyond my wildest dreams!

Today, Lisa lives devoted to God and motherhood. Her life is a testimony of the exceeding greatness of God's power to free us from our bondages and make us holy and blameless in His sight.

I used to feel responsible to make the lost come to Jesus, but I'm learning my responsibility is simply to share God's truths, pray for a response, and then wait in a spirit of praise. Through this experience with Lisa, God showed me that nothing and no one could stop Him from unfolding and fulfilling His plan. There's no place, no person God's mercy cannot reach. When I trust in His sovereign time and ways, I enjoy greater peace and joy in my life while watching in amazement how He saves lost souls.

Discussion Questions

1. If God is in control of everything, does that mean Christians can sit back and not bother to reach out and love others? Why or why not? Can you support your answers with Scriptures?

2. Explain how Sue's responses to Lisa demonstrated Sue's trust in God's ability to work out His will. If you were Sue, how might you have responded?

3. How can you know when to press in to share God's truth with an unbeliever or when to back off?

4. It is the Holy Spirit, not we, who converts an individual. However, we are called to be His ambassadors. How did the Holy Spirit use Sue's message, her personality, her life?

5. How is the Holy Spirit using your unique personality, your unique message, your life to evangelize?

Kindness has converted more sinners than zeal,
eloquence, or learning. —*Henrietta Mears*

Loving a Jehovah's Witness

Joanne Southerland as told to Pamela Enderby

"Do not let any unwholesome talk come out of your
mouths, but only what is helpful" (Ephesians 4:29).

While interviewing 19-year-old Tina for a nanny position, I quickly discovered she was passionate about nurturing kids. She seemed perfect for my five children, ages 12, 9, 8, 3, and 18 months. Then she dropped the bomb. She confessed to being a Jehovah's Witness, fourth-generation no less!

A few years earlier, I had delved into studying other religions and had learned how to share the Gospel with people tangled in cults. Eventually, literature on Christianity, Mormons, New Age, and Jehovah's Witnesses filled my bookshelves.

Now, pondering this opportunity to put my knowledge to work excited me, but it also instigated negative comments from my well-meaning friends. "I don't think it's safe leaving your kids with a Jehovah's Witness. She'll share her beliefs and confuse them."

Rather than caving in to their gloomy forecasts, I turned to God's Word. "God did not give us a spirit of fear, but of power, love, and a sound mind" (2 Timothy 1:7). This Scripture boosted my faith, and with Tina's promise not to proselytize my kids, I hired her for three days a week.

Soon thereafter, I discovered book knowledge wasn't enough. I made some mistakes trying to put it to work and win Tina to Christ. Although at times I was insensitive to the Holy Spirit, I gained experience that taught me valuable tips for witnessing.

One sunny afternoon, a few months after I had hired Tina, she appeared in the doorway of my office, unloading her frustrations. "A lot of books call the Jehovah's Witness religion a cult," she blurted. "They're written by people who used to be Jehovah's Witnesses. They're mad at us," her voice swelled. "They write lies about our religion."

My heart began to race with excitement. I pushed my papers aside and cleared my throat, preparing to pounce on this witnessing opportunity. It seemed obvious to me that Tina needed to hear, right then, basic Christian doctrine. First, salvation comes by grace through faith alone, apart from human merit. Consequently, activities in God's service and energetic witnessing cannot measure up to the righteousness of Christ assigned to all who hear His Word and believe.

Strangely, I felt God nudging me to silence.

Nevertheless, I plunged in when Tina ended her spiel. Now, looking squarely into her soft blue eyes, I began, "Thank you, Tina, for sharing your beliefs with me. I'm very interested in your religion. As a matter of fact, I've read books about it, and I agree it's a lot different from mine." Tina unfolded her arms, her body relaxed. She appeared ready to hear the truth about the Jehovah's Witness errors. So I began firing information and questions.

"Do you know the Jehovah's Witness Watch Tower is a man-made organization that governs your religion? They throw out doctrine again and again and replace it with new doctrine called 'New Light.' For example, the Watchtower's first president, Charles Russell, published a series of books called *Studies in the Scriptures*. It teaches that Christ returned in 1874. Then the Watchtower abandoned that doctrine and started teaching that Christ's invisible second presence began in 1914." I ignored Tina's glare.

"Russell also taught that the resurrection of dead Christians occurred in 1878. Today, the Watchtower teaches they resurrected in 1918." With my voice rising, I gulped, "Tina, how can you be sure that in 25 more years, Jehovah's Witnesses won't also reject the claims of their current president, Milton Henschel?" Tina's eyes grew wider and her lips tightened.

Tina rose from her chair. "It sounds as if you believe everything those books say about us," she snapped. Unloading my knowledge too soon seemed to undo weeks of relationship building.

I had pushed Tina too far, trying to get her to think clearly and objectively. "What do I say now?" I prayed, silently. My knowledge hardly impressed her. I should have heeded Paul's inspired words, "Walk in wisdom toward those who are outside, redeeming the time. Let your speech always be with grace, seasoned with salt, that you may know how you ought to answer each one" (Colossians 4:5-6).

Frustrated and unsure of what to say next, I quietly asked God to guide me. Now, I would patiently heed His course of action.

First, I realized the need to apologize. Without compromising my beliefs, I could still show Tina kindness. Remembering that Jehovah's Witnesses don't understand God as One who gives and keeps promises, immediately I turned a corner with our conversation.

"Tina, do you mind if I share a personal story with you about God's faithfulness?" I asked, gingerly. Tina nodded and sank back into her chair, arms clasped tight again.

"One day, at Wal-Mart, I left my wallet on top of a gas pump. It was filled with my kids' pictures, credit cards, and money. Of course I panicked when I realized it was missing. So I prayed, asking God to protect it and somehow get it back into my safekeeping." I paused. Tina flashed me a curious look. Her square, broad shoulders leaned forward, anticipating the rest of the story.

Two days later, Wal-Mart called. A store employee had found my kids' pictures and driver's license on a shelf crowded with toiletries. "God is so good! He's trustworthy and loving. He even takes care of little things, like my kids' pictures."

From that day on I continued to take a different approach with Tina. I remember reading about an ex-Jehovah's Witness applauding Christians for their faith-filled prayers. "I had never heard anybody pray like a born-again Christian." It helped unlock his heart to salvation.

So now, when Tina and I sit at the kitchen table, discussing my kids' daily activities, I usually end our conversation by praying boldly and out loud for their safety, health, and friendships.

Tina also observes that I begin each day with Bible study. Before entering my bedroom and shutting the door, I tell her, "God's Word is full of wisdom. I read it for guidance and it gives me strength for the day."

Randall Watters, ex-Jehovah's Witness and former Watchtower headquarters staffer, comments, "People are usually drawn toward a more positive outlook on things, and if you have nothing better to offer than criticism of the Watchtower, they won't see any point in leaving because what you have to offer is no more attractive than what they have."

As I gain Tina's trust, occasionally, she voices disillusionment with the Watchtower. She is slowly realizing that this "God organization" is really a human organization and that her world will not fall apart if it is wrong. When Tina speaks critically of the organization or its people, my goal is to encourage her toward more positive thoughts and to gain confidence in her own thinking apart from the Watchtower mindset.

I am called to evangelize with words that build up, encourage, and edify (Ephesians 4:29). Speaking words that are only positive and not negative will be a gift to Tina. I'm learning I cannot argue Tina into faith in Jesus; it is the Holy Spirit who convicts.

The Witnesses offer a strong sense of community, a caring atmosphere, security, and status. If Tina renounces her faith, she can be excommunicated from her family and church and lose all those things.

Considering this high price, Tina must see and feel something more than the Watchtower offers. She must experience genuine Christian love regardless of what she believes. It's essential that I show Biblical, agape love—love that is active and selfless (Romans 5:8).

For this reason, I now treat Tina as if she were one of my family members. While working with me, she not only hears about the love of Christ, but also sees genuine humility. My willingness to listen to her and try to understand her is building our friendship. Tina is growing to believe I have her best interests in mind. If someday she considers leaving the Jehovah's Witnesses, I will invite her to live with us.

Henrietta Mears, outstanding Christian education teacher and writer and one who helped establish Gospel Light Publications, is known as one who wasn't afraid to trust God no matter how difficult the circumstances. She says, "Kindness has converted more sinners than zeal, eloquence, or learning."

Tina needs my fervent prayers. I don't tell her that I'm praying for her, that I feel sorry for her, or that she's brainwashed. Witnesses, like Tina, have strong egos and quickly take offense to a condescending attitude.

God is bigger than the Jehovah of the Watchtower. As I pray, I believe Jesus will soften Tina's heart and open her mind to see the empty deception of her religion. I often use these points when praying for Tina:

- open her spiritual eyes (2 Corinthians 4:4)
- set her free from spiritual captivity (2 Timothy 2:25-26)
- give her ears to hear (Matthew 13:15), faith to believe (Acts 20:21), and the will to respond (Romans 10:9)
- send people to witness to her (Matthew 9:28)
- give me creative ways to continue building a caring relationship (1 Corinthians 9:22)

I'm praying that God will show Tina only He can meet her needs, not the Watchtower community. He will create a new hunger in her for something better. The battle is spiritual and must be fought in God's strength, depending on the Word and through prayer. He is the One that draws men and women to Jesus (John 6:44).

Discussion Questions

1. Personal fears and prejudices often hinder our evangelistic efforts toward people lost in false religions. Explain those this story describes and perhaps those you struggle with.

2. In what ways did Joanne witness effectively to Tina? What turned out to be an ineffective witness?

3. How was Joanne's method of using her book knowledge detrimental to witnessing?

4. Refer to Ephesians 4:29. When evangelizing, why is this a significant thing to practice?

5. Do you want to better understand and reach out to Jehovah's Witnesses, Mormons, and others? Explore the following resources:

Books: *Mormons Answered Verse by Verse* by David Reed and John Farkas.

Answering Jehovah's Witnesses Subject by Subject by David Reed.

Reasoning From the Scriptures With the Jehovah's Witnesses by Ron Rhodes.

Pamphlet: *Christianity, Cults and Religions* (Compares 17 religions and cults with Biblical Christianity) by Rose Publishing, 4455 Torrance Blvd., Suite 259; Torrance, CA

DVD: *In the Name of Jehovah: Understanding Jehovah's Witnesses*, a 90-minute DVD produced by the Interfaith Evangelism Team of the North American Mission Board. It explores and dispels the fear of sharing your faith with those who come falsely in the name of God. For more information, visit www.namb.net/interfaith, or call 866-407-6262.

~

Obstacle Seven: I'm Fearful of Getting Rejected.

"Surely God is my salvation; I will trust and not be afraid. The Lord, the Lord is my strength and my song; he has become my salvation"

(Isaiah 12:2).

As skillful as a surgeon must be in using the scalpel,
so must the soul-winner be in witnessing.
—Dr. Robert Lee

Cyber Outreach

Gerald Boyd as told to Pamela Enderby

"Each day proclaim the good news that he saves. Publish the glorious deeds among the nations" (Psalm 96:3 NLT).

On the Internet I have communicated the love and saving grace of Jesus Christ to people all over the globe. Advanced technology makes it possible for me to strike up a conversation with a housewife in Toronto, a teen Satanist in Germany, an atheist in New York, or a seeker in London.

One evening, I went to the chat lines and found a lonely young woman searching for happiness. "I think I am happy, but there are times I am not sure," she stated. I instantly e-mailed her to see if I could be of help.

I learned she went to church as a child, but never had a personal experience with God. I responded, "That's really sad. Without His presence in our lives we just exist. God created us to worship him." I inquired, "Do you have a Bible?"

"No, but I've read it before. It's all mumbo jumbo to me. I can't understand the words," she wrote.

"You owe it to yourself to spend a few dollars and get a copy of an easy-to-read translation, such as the *New Living Translation.*"

When she told me she was a nurse in Buffalo, New York, I encouraged her, "You're in a wonderful position to help people on their way out of this life with just a kind word or Scripture. It would give them peace of mind."

I gave her Scriptures to read: Romans 3:23; 6:23; 10:9-10; 1 Corinthians 2:14; 1 John 1:9; Revelation 3:20; 2 Corinthians 5:17. "These verses will show you how to come into a personal relationship with Jesus Christ. That's different from attending a church. It isn't religion we want, but a personal relationship with Christ. Makes sense, doesn't it?"

"Yes," she replied.

After we chatted some more online about her family and religious background, I shared John 3:16, "For God so loved the world he gave His only begotten son, that whosoever believes in Him should not perish but have eternal life."

"I know that one. I learned it in Bible school when I was little," she commented. "But I've never been baptized."

"Do you believe in God and His son Jesus Christ who came to die for our sins?" I asked. "He gave His life for all sinners and all we have to do is accept Him as our Savior. He's the Forgiver of our sins. I John 1:9 says, 'If we confess our sins He is faithful and just to forgive us our sins and cleanse us from all unrighteousness.'" I paused a moment and wrote, "Would you accept that?"

I waited for her usual instant reply, but this time she kept me waiting. "Do you believe this is the truth?" I queried and waited.

"Yes, this is true," she confessed.

"Would you like to have a personal relationship with God tonight? I can write out a prayer of confession and you can tell me if it meets the desire of your heart."

"O.K.," she responded.

"In the privacy of your home you can come into fellowship with the lover of your soul, Jesus Christ, God's Son. I'll write out a prayer … hold."

"Heavenly Father, I come to you as a sinner, for Your Word says that all have sinned and come short of the glory of God. Forgive me, I pray. Receive me, as Your child. I want to serve You, and obey Your Word. I thank You for dying on the cross for my sins. Make me the person You would have me to be. In Jesus name I pray, Amen."

After giving her a few minutes to read through the prayer, I asked, "Does this meet the desire of your heart?"

"Yes, thank you."

"God knows your thoughts, and the desire of your heart. Welcome into God's family of believers."

"By the way, my first name is Jerry … yours?"

"Chrissy," she replied.

"God bless you, Chrissy. That is the greatest prayer you will ever pray."

"Thank you. Maybe that is what I needed."

"Second Corinthians 5:17 says, 'Therefore, if any man be in Christ he becomes a totally new person. Old things are passed away, and behold all things become new.' Your life will begin to change from this moment on."

Before signing off, Chrissy divulged her home city and zip code. I identified some names and addresses of churches where she could hear about God and learn from His Word.

Another young man I witnessed to on the Internet was a Satanist who wrote, "I have had much Christian information passed on to me from countless years of Sunday school and church. I looked at different sects—Catholic, Baptist, you name it. I have come to realize it's all false information. I looked at the Hindu faith, Buddhist faith, and Zen.

174

Now, I believe Satanism to be the only true faith. If there truly was a God or Holy Spirit, don't you think He would have struck me down long ago?"

After conversing with him at length, this hardened rebellious sinner opened his heart and received Jesus Christ as his Savior. Now he says, "God has changed my life and given me an inner peace that I had never known." Later he wrote, "I truly did ask Jesus to come into my life and I am happy now! I owe it all to you. You have shown me the way and for that I will forever be indebted to you." This fellow quit the band he was playing with, changed his screen name, and is reading the Word.

By God's grace, I've encouraged others who are struggling with pornography, dabbling in astrology, or contemplating suicide by sharing Scriptures with them.

Without a doubt, Internet evangelism is the most exciting ministry I have ever had in all of my life. And I've had a lot because I'm an 82-year-old retired minister! I can't thank the Lord enough for allowing me to serve this way at my age.

Discussion Questions

1. Discuss the advantages and disadvantages of witnessing on the web. How might online evangelism help you overcome your witnessing fears?

2. What key Scriptures helped Gerald witness effectively to the nurse writing from Buffalo? Consider memorizing Scriptures to use in witnessing.

2. What are some leading questions to initiate meaningful conversations?

3. As a "cyber-missionary," how is it possible to show genuine concern?

Never object to the intense sensitivity of the Spirit of
God in you when He is instructing you down to the
smallest detail. —Oswald Chambers

Expect the Unexpected

Greg Hughes as told to Pamela Enderby

"Oh, the depth of the riches of the wisdom and knowledge
of God!" (Romans 11:33).

Driving down Highway 70, a shaft of light streaming
from a convenience store pierced the black sky and arrested
my attention. As I drove closer to it, I sensed a mysterious
tugging, wooing me to stop. I checked my fuel gauge.
"Nope, half full, no need to stop," I said to myself, and continued full speed ahead.

Strange enough, my heart started to race. Either this is a
bad case of indigestion from all the junk food I've eaten or
maybe I'm over exhausted. I had just finished preaching
five consecutive nights to crowds of noisy, rambunctious
teens.

With my last ounce of energy, I glanced at my watch.
"It's 1:00 a. m. I'm tired, my nerves are shot, and I've got
10 more hours of driving before I get home," I growled.
My heart continued to race. "God, what's going on?" I

prayed. Silence met me. Out of curiosity and for my physical well-being, I took the next exit and headed toward the store.

As I entered Cal's Mart, I spotted a tall thin man standing behind the counter. We looked at each other, but neither of us said a word. I paced up and down the food aisle, not knowing what else to do. I'm sure I looked foolish.

"Could he be the reason I'm here?" I muttered to myself. But I was fearful of talking to him and risk sounding weird.

Trying to move quickly for the door, I could barely lift my legs because they felt heavy, as if weighted down with bricks. I strained forward with each step. That's when I got a clue. I turned around.

The teens had heard me challenge them over and over, "God will use you anywhere, anytime to share your faith. Be sensitive and obedient to His ways. Don't be afraid!"

With His presence resting upon me, I was willing and ready. Now, what am I supposed to do? I wondered.

Reaching deep into my pockets, I slowly walked toward the skinny guy. "Hey, you might think I'm weird or something …" I cleared my throat while nervously tapping my foot. "But when I was driving by, my heart started racing." I held my hand above my heart mimicking its throbbing motion. "I think God wanted me to come back and talk to you. So, here I am." I cleared my throat again, stalling for time, hoping he would say something to ease my embarrassment. "I really don't know what else to say," I muttered and smiled. We stared at each other without speaking a word. I wanted to run for the door.

"I've been asking God to prove He's real." His words split the uncomfortable silence. "I've been having these real bad feelings lately, and I'm getting angry a lot. I asked God to either help me or leave me alone." His unkempt hair fell in his eyes as he looked down, fidgeting with the strings hanging from his utility apron.

I breathed a huge sigh of relief, leaned closer to him, and continued, my heart still racing. "When you go home tonight, take a few minutes to tell God what's bothering you. He wants to hear from you. He loves you." He looked up at me with a shy grin.

"You think God hears me?"

"Sure, He does," I answered. "God loves you and wants to help you." Then another long, disturbing silence met us.

Hoping I had finished this mission, I turned to leave. But God's gentle voice stopped me. "Pray with him." Slowly, I turned around.

"Hey, I'd like to pray for you … right now." My words seemed to come easier.

"Well," he said, hesitantly. "I guess it won't hurt." I detected a glimmer of hope in his voice.

With our heads bowed, I said a simple prayer, thanking God for this young man's life. I also asked God to reveal His love to him and help him work through his anger. I purposefully didn't press him for a decision because I felt his heart needed more preparation, more softening. Ongoing prayer for him would pave the way to increase God's work in his life.

I left the gas station filled with peace. An abundance of stars filled the sky that night, providing another astounding display of God's divine undertaking.

Just as I told the kids, no one can plan, figure, or predict the Holy Spirit's moving. When the Holy Spirit is ready to minister, we must make room for Him to come in anytime, anywhere, anyplace, even if it means losing a few hours of sleep, and even if it feels like we're buttonholing a stranger.

Hopefully, I'll be more cooperative the next time. Submitting to the Spirit's unexpected ways ultimately brings sheer satisfaction.

Discussion Questions

1. This true story models confrontational outreach. Explain its positives and negatives.

2. How did Greg use extreme sensitivity in this situation?

3. In *Life-Style Evangelism*, Joseph Aldrich states, "The vast majority do not become Christians by confrontational, stranger-to-stranger evangelism." If this is true, why should we still remain open to this method?

4. Greg overcame his fear of looking foolish and getting rejected. How did his honest, vulnerable approach minister to the cashier?

5. Greg finally understood it was God leading him to this outreach. Do you think it's always possible to know when God is about to use you? Why or why not?

6. How might you prepare yourself for an "unexpected" outreach encounter?

God does not turn us into spiritual agents but into spiritual messengers ... the message must be a part of us. Our lives must be a holy example of the reality of our message. —Oswald Chambers

Goodie Two Shoes Shares the Good News

Stephanie Fridley as told to Pamela Enderby

"Don't let anyone look down on you because you are young, but set an example" (1 Timothy 4:12).

Growing up in a neighborhood full of unruly boys put my faith to the test! The troublemakers ridiculed me for refusing to join in their shenanigans. When I wouldn't throw eggs at houses, put rotten tomatoes in mailboxes, and steal goodies from Sam's ice cream truck, they cackled, "There goes Goodie Two Shoes!"

I scolded them anyway. "You shouldn't be doing that." As a young child I developed a strong sense of right and wrong: "Do unto others as you would have them do unto you."

"It's no big deal," sneered David, the ringleader, waving a stolen ice cream bar in my face. "They only cost fifteen cents."

Most of the time I felt disgusted with their behavior, but sometimes I secretly wished to join them. I wondered if their mischievous adventures would liven up the stale moments in my 11-year-old life. At times, I also longed to feel their acceptance. But my strong conviction to set a good example before these rebel rousers deterred me. Equally powerful was my fear of getting caught and suffering my parents' wrath.

David's father, baldheaded and decorated with tattoos, usually gave me the most grief. Like a giant Goliath, he taunted me for devoting my summers to missionary work. Whenever he saw me dressed up, going to church, he'd cackle those familiar stinging words, "There goes Goodie Two Shoes again." It didn't take long before the whole gang of neighborhood bullies joined in. I detested it. Like sharp arrows, their words stuck deep in my heart.

The put downs humiliated me, but I refused to strike back, at least, when I was in their presence. Instead, at bedtime, I cried and vented. "Oh, God, You see all the grief I'm taking. Get 'im!"

Two years later, David and his family moved and most of the ridicule stopped. Relieved, I figured I'd never see David or his family again.

I didn't see that bunch of troublemakers for many years, although their faces continued to show up in my mind during my prayer times. I even had my friends praying for them.

With time and prayer, the pain their ridicule had caused dulled. When memories of David, his mean buddies, and his dad came to mind, I didn't feel angry anymore. That must be why Jesus instructs us to pray for our enemies. I discovered it's difficult to stay mad at someone you're praying for.

During my college years, while living on a skimpy budget, my close missionary friend invited me to her wedding. I had planned to go, but only if I had a free place to stay. After learning about David's family living near my friend, I mustered up enough courage to call them. With open arms, the entire family received me, and with their warm reception, more answers to prayers began unfolding.

Upon my arrival, I met David, then a marine. The scrawny, 11-year-old bully had grown into a young man with bulging muscles, head to toe. He happened to be home on furlough for a few weeks. Whenever our paths crossed in the kitchen, usually at mealtimes, I deliberately kept my conversations with him brief and upbeat to avoid any possibility of upsetting him.

The day before returning home, David stopped me in the kitchen. "I have to drive to southern California tomorrow. Why not ride with me?" I couldn't resist his offer. It was a cheap way home that fit my budget.

The following morning, I hurled my suitcase into David's old van and climbed in. For miles he shared lighthearted talk about his military experiences sprinkled with hopes and dreams about his future. I relaxed while David's chatter filled hours of travel time.

Then suddenly, David turned serious. "You know, Stephanie," he said, with his eyes smiling at me. "I just want to say I'm sorry for making fun of you when we were young. And I'm really sorry for calling you Goodie Two Shoes. I made your life miserable just because you didn't want to get into trouble. And I shouldn't have teased you about God. Please forgive me."

My mouth dropped. I stared at him, stunned. "Oh yeah?" I finally squeaked out. I could tell David had changed. After listening to him for miles, he sounded thoughtful, even gentle, but I never expected to hear him say, "I'm sorry," for rude childhood remarks.

"Ahhh, David," I stammered, fidgeting with the clasp on my seat belt. "Why are you apologizing? I mean, I don't

182

want to sound religious, but you sound different. Have you had an experience with God or something?" I couldn't think of any other reason for his kindness.

I swallowed hard, silently rehearsing a verbal scourging, the kind he used to give me when we were kids.

"You know, Stephanie," he said, slowly, methodically, "I've started reading the Bible once in a while because I know that's the right thing to do." He glanced at me with one of his piercing looks, smiled thoughtfully, and continued. "I'm not going to church yet, but I want to know God better. You know, like the way you know him." David's tender words felt like warm oil washing over me.

"Would you tell me more about God?"

I couldn't tell him enough, fast enough! For miles, my stomach turned somersaults as I shared my spiritual journey. I explained how I came to know God as my personal Savior, how I'm growing intimate with Him, and learning to trust Him as my best friend.

As David listened carefully and respectfully, the wall around his heart fell just like the light raindrops on our windshield. When I finished, he shared a watershed of memories, including his past joys and sorrows, disappointments and victories. Then he admitted his need for God. He acknowledged God could heal his past and give him direction for his future, yet he wasn't ready to completely surrender.

I silently prayed, "Oh, Lord, thank you for giving me courage to live my life before David, honoring you. For helping me set an example when he desperately needed to see some resemblance of You living through me. And thank you for softening David's heart. Help him to receive Your love and forgiveness."

Hearing David express his lostness triggered painful childhood memories of when he picked on me. Tears trickled down my cheeks. But now, instead of anger, compassion gripped my heart. I saw more than just a mean little boy who had hurt my feelings. I saw David becoming a miracle of God's grace.

When we reached our destination that evening, David and I promised to keep in touch with one another. We exchanged sweet good-byes. My heart was beaming; I was smiling from ear to ear.

Because of God's mercy, He used our reunion to take David one step closer to Himself. I trust God's faithfulness will continue to show him the Truth. For me, David's kind words helped heal my wounds, and I also felt God's affirmation for staying true to Him as a child.

Today, when David comes to mind, I hear myself uttering that simple prayer that worked so well as a child, "Oh God...get 'im." But, now, I'm praying with a new heart. It's full of peace and pure joy that desires only the best for my new friend.

Discussion Questions

1. In I Timothy 4:12, *The Message* reads, "Get the word out. Teach all these things. And don't let anyone put you down because you're young. Teach believers with your life: by word, by demeanor, by love, by faith, by integrity." In your own words, share what it means to "teach believers with your life."

2. If our children are setting an example to others in attitude, actions, and habits how might that look? How can we encourage them to do so?

3. How can we help our children overcome their outreach fears so they stand firm in their faith when they are ridiculed?

4. In what way(s) do you think your life reflects a Christ-like message?

If you believe that blind men are falling into the
furnace, is there any conceivable way you can hold
your peace? —D. James Kennedy

Tracting For Jesus

Debbie Stephanatos as told to Pam Enderby

"I heard the voice of the Lord saying, "Whom shall I send?
... And I said, 'Here am I. Send me!'" (Isaiah 6:8).

My eyes roamed the seats of the crowded commuter
train in Manhattan. I wanted a quiet spot to sit and unwind
after a hectic workday.

As I shuffled down the aisle, peculiar looking booklets
spotted the seats. They piqued my interest. Setting my
briefcase down, I picked one up. Silly looking cartoon
characters illustrated a story about Jesus. I had seen this
kind of propaganda before, placed in public restrooms and
the library. Who's invading my territory again with their
crazy religion? Irritation overruled my weariness. I
marched out of the train determined to find the intruder.

A quick look around Huntington Station revealed more
obnoxious pamphlets and the culprit—a young man standing among the crowd, smiling and passing out tracts.

"Excuse me, sir." I said, thrusting my hand on my hip. "Who do you think you are trying to push your religion on me?" I spewed a string of accusations, attacking his character and the foolish booklets. I could feel my body temperature rising.

The religious fanatic didn't flinch. As a matter of fact, his calm, quiet nature only annoyed me more. Red-faced and puffing, I threw the pamphlet down and whisked off.

Two years later and nine months pregnant, I experienced another divine appointment. While retreating on the couch and browsing the TV Guide for an entertaining game show to watch to help alleviate my discomfort, I spotted *The 700 Club*. It sounded like a good possibility, so I flicked it on. At first, the show's host sounded like one of those television evangelists my co-workers had warned me of. They advised, "Don't trust them! They're phonies."

As I strained to get up to turn off the television, a strange thing happened. Ben Kinchlow, the TV host, stopped me. "Don't touch the dial," he said, and he began to pray. His prayer revealed the deep longings of my heart; it seemed he could read my mind.

Day after day, I eagerly turned on *The 700 Club* to hear more. The truth about God's unconditional love and forgiveness penetrated my heart. *Wow! Maybe God is real.*

All my life I had been running from God. Now, my wall of defensiveness began to crumble, as did my fears and doubts about the reality of God. Because of God's faithfulness, nothing could separate me from His tenacious love.

After my son was born, I had to return to work, and the surrogate grandmother I had hired decided to move upstate. With her resignation, I felt a lot of anxiety. That's when God used a Christian woman's sensitivity and obedience to take me one step closer to salvation.

One morning she called me at work to tell me she believes God answers prayer and that He would provide another caretaker if we asked Him. On the spot, at that moment, she began to pray! My heart had softened enough to keep from hanging up on her or lashing out at her for being "religiously intrusive." Still, I feared the embarrassment of my co-workers finding out I was participating in prayer, so I simply acknowledged her with "yep," "o.k." and "sure."

God was silently planning a wonderful surprise of love. The next day, God answered her prayer by sending me a woman who became not only my child's caretaker but also my spiritual mentor.

Shortly after, with my faith awakened, I fully surrendered myself to the One who never gave up on me. At last, my tangled life began to straighten. Attending Bible studies strengthened and encouraged my faith and my prayer life grew rapidly. What is more amazing, I began to share my faith in public!

"Let's hand out tracts at the train station before work," my neighbor and friend David suggested.

"What if I offend someone?" I cringed. Flashbacks of angry thoughts and words I expressed toward others who had tried sharing their faith with me flooded my mind. I didn't want anyone calling me "crazy."

I put David off as long as possible until finally I got tired of his pressing. "O.K., I'll pray about it," I said.

Soon after, I received God's gentle reproof through His Word. He showed me that keeping my faith private didn't agree with His plan and that He already had provided all I needed to speak on His behalf. That included spiritual braveness and boldness. "You will receive power when the Holy Spirit has come upon you; and you shall be My witnesses (Acts 1:8 NASB).

Each morning I joined David before going to work to pass out tracts at Huntington Station. The very thing that once had infuriated me now invigorated me. My earnest desire to share God's love helped put tracts in the hands of multitudes of business executives whom I called, "three-piece suiters." They boarded the Manhattan train to commute to the World Trade Center on Long Island. Most of the time, I felt God's peaceful presence resting over me like a blanket.

Several years later, on September 11, 2001, disaster struck New York City. A terrorist plane crashed into the World Trade Center, leaving thousands dead. Perhaps many of those "three-piece suiters" had received my tracts. I can still see images of them marching across my mind. I wonder how many read the tracts? I like to think some of them are now standing before Jesus because they trusted in Him for salvation.

When that extraordinary crisis hit New York City, no able-bodied citizen felt he had any right to rest till he had done all he could to save as many as he could. Likewise, the world lives in a time of spiritual crisis. William Barclay stated, "The possession of the good news of the Gospel involves the obligation to share it." It seems that no Christian should rest until every unbeliever is given the opportunity to be rescued.

We should be more like Isaiah. When he saw the extraordinary crisis around him, he couldn't help but respond, "Lord, here am I; send me." More and more, I discover my heart saying the same thing. Practically everywhere I go I see someone in need of salvation. Passing out tracts is my favorite way of sharing the Good News.

Discussion Questions

1. What was Debbie's biggest fear about handing out tracts? Have you ever received a tract? What was your response?

2. David Buttram, president of Gospel Tract Harvester, states, "Gospel tracts are still the most cost-effective way to present the Word of God in a tasteful and attractive manner." Discuss the advantages and disadvantages of using tracts.

3. Brainstorm various places and other opportunities for passing out tracts.

4. Taking initiative and being bold is not natural for most of us. The disciples prayed for boldness (Acts 4:29). Take a moment to ask God for courage to share His love with a dying world.

The most effective means of evangelism is personal
relationship witnessing. —Ron D. Dempsey

A Long Journey to the Christmas Coffee

Lisa Bozarth as told to Pamela Enderby

"I am your God. I will strengthen you and help you; I will uphold you with my righteous right hand" (Isaiah 41:10).

For nine years I failed to touch a single soul in my neighborhood. Now I was moving to another town feeling guilty and irresponsible. When I confessed my negligence to a friend, rather than scold me, she exhorted me, "Moving into your new neighborhood will give you a fresh start. Why not host an evangelistic Christmas coffee after you settle in?"

My journey to a Christmas outreach launched quickly and unexpectedly. After settling into our new neighborhood, I met Christie, another home-school mom. While our kids took Spanish lessons together, we shared heartfelt needs and prayed for each other. I learned that Christie also desired to share God's love with her neighbors, so I suggested we co-host an evangelistic Christmas coffee. We prayed about the idea for three months.

Then December arrived. Would we co-host a Christmas coffee? We were reluctant. Christie had been taught never to share the Gospel without knowing someone intimately. I was discouraged because I had not yet met any of my neighbors in spite of my prayers that God would open doors for us. "Christie," I said, "Let's wait until next Christmas to have an outreach. Right now it's probably time to keep sowing seeds of prayer."

We searched Scriptures relating to evangelism, secretly hoping they would support our desire to put off the outreach. Christie found Scriptures that encouraged believers to witness boldly while God impressed upon me, "Now is the time to share the Gospel." One morning, during her quiet time, Christie just happened to read Psalm 40:9-10: "I proclaim righteousness in the great assembly; I do not seal my lips, as you know, O Lord. I do not hide your righteousness in my heart; I speak of your faithfulness and salvation. I do not conceal your love and your truth from the great assembly." I realized the great assembly could be our neighborhood.

God's Word pushed us forward, but only for a short distance before fear of persecution began terrorizing me. That's when I slammed on my outreach brakes. What if someone throws eggs at my house or tries to hurt my kids after they find out I'm a Christian? Again, turning to God's Word relieved my fears and loosed the enemy's clamp. "Do not fear, for I am with you; do not be dismayed, for I am your God. I will strengthen you and help you; I will uphold you with my righteous right hand" (Isaiah 41:10).

When I began to prepare the Christmas coffee devotional, more fear surfaced. Sharing the gospel with a group of unbelievers seemed more frightening than the thought of getting stuck in an elevator. Then God's still, small voice sounded again, "I am the same yesterday, today, and forever." He reminded me of Scriptures that tell how He rescued the Israelites from their enemy by parting the Red Sea. If I was willing to step out in faith, He promised to rescue me, too.

With God's Word now planted firmly in Christie's heart, she assured me, "We're not to worry about how people are going to respond. It's God's job to draw them, not ours."

Two weeks before the event, weak-kneed yet excited, we hand-delivered thirty-two Christmas coffee invitations to our neighbors. To my relief, everyone welcomed us warmly and expressed a desire to meet their neighbors. We also bridged the beginnings of new friendships as we chatted with a woman recovering from a double mastectomy, a single mom, and several elderly women. As Christi and I continued to meet to pray for our neighbors, God enlarged our hearts with His love for them and increased our confidence in what He was doing.

Finally, the evening of the Christmas coffee arrived. The blazing fireplace cast shadows of dancing flames reflecting the excitement in our hearts. While I nervously bustled about straightening bows on our Christmas tree and lighting scented candles, Christie stopped me. "Let's pray. I'm scared," she whispered. Prayer quieted our hearts. Finally, the doorbell rang and we ushered in our first guest.

Christie introduced the evening with an icebreaker, a giant stride for a shy person, and I confidently delivered the devotional, including an invitation to accept Christ. The fear and doubt that had badgered me throughout this journey had completely vanished. Near the end of the evening, I proposed we meet again to possibly explore more of the Bible. "Anyone interested?" I asked. No one seemed enthused, but neither did they stampede for the door. Instead they lingered late into the evening, chatting, admiring Christmas decorations, and munching Christmas goodies.

Inspired by our Christmas outreach, Christie and I decided we should keep on praying for our neighbors. About one year later, I led our first women's neighborhood Bible study. They included the women who attended our evangelistic Christmas coffee.

Plans for Your Own Christmas Coffee
Christmas Coffee Hostess
1. Invite three times as many neighbors as your room will comfortably seat.
2. Hand out invitations two weeks in advance.
a. Include the date, time, place, and your phone number. Also indicate clearly that a friend will be sharing some inspiring thoughts about Christmas. Ask them to RSVP by phone or email to get a good idea of the number of people to expect.
b. If you do not know your neighbors' names or addresses, you may choose to hand deliver the invitations. Point out your home, underscoring the fact that it's a neighborhood gathering. If you mail your invitations, allow time so they will arrive at least two weeks before your coffee. (Most coffees are held the first two weeks of December.)
3. Try to arrange a time with your speaker to pray together and encourage your Christian friends to pray for this outreach.
4. When guests arrive, serve finger foods and provide nametags if appropriate.
5. To help everyone get acquainted stimulate conversation about personal topics such as home, family, jobs. Also, I've used this idea: "One of the things I find enjoyable and interesting is learning about other people's Christmas traditions. Let's share some of our traditions, such as your favorite foods, family customs, or Christmas plans this year."
6. Place chairs for easy conversation (not rows). Set up additional chairs as needed.
7. Place speaker in a central location, but not in front of a window.
8. Introduce your speaker about 30 minutes after everyone arrives.

Christmas Coffee Speaker
1. Find out about her neighborhood.
a. Approximate age of neighbors
b. Any uniqueness about the neighborhood
c. What will they wear?
d. Any special prayer requests

2. Practice your talk often and even aloud. The entire presentation should range from 10-15 minutes.

3. At the end of your talk lead into a prayer with something like this: "If you desire to receive Christ, we need to tell Him so. For those who wish to receive Christ, silently pray with me as I pray aloud. Let's bow our heads."

"Heavenly Father, thank you for loving me. I am grateful that Your Son Jesus came to earth as a baby, grew to be a man and died on the cross for my sins. I want to open the door of my heart and receive You as my Savior and Lord. Please take control of my life. In the name of Jesus, Amen."

Sample Time Schedule
Example: Morning coffee from 9 a.m.-11 a.m.
9:00-9:30 Arrive and have refreshments
9:30-10:00 Sharing time with neighbors
10:00-10:30 Speaker and prayer invitation
10:30-11:00 More coffee and food

Discussion Questions

1. In Luke 10, Jesus sent out the seventy-two disciples two-by-two. In Acts 13:1-3, the church in Antioch sent Paul and Barnabus on their first missionary journey. Why do you think they went in pairs?

2. What benefits did Lisa and Christie experience by working together?

3. Ask the Lord who He might want you to join hearts with to prepare and plan an evangelistic Christmas coffee.

www.ingramcontent.com/pod-product-compliance
Lightning Source LLC
LaVergne TN
LVHW051052080426
835508LV00019B/1832